Quick & Easy Woodworking Projects

Handyman Club Library™

Handyman Club of America
Minnetonka, Minnesota

Quick & Easy Woodworking Projects

Printed in 2010.

CREDITS

Tom Carpenter
Creative Director

Mark Johanson
Book Products Development Manager

Chris Marshall
Editor, Series Coordinator

Dan Cary
Photo Production Coordinator

Steve Anderson
Senior Editorial Assistant, Copywriter

Marti Naughton
Series Design, Art Direction & Production

Kim Bailey
Photographer

Rod Mechem, John Nadeau
Project Builders

John Drigot
Technical Illustrations

Brad Classon
Production Assistance

ISBN 10: 1-58159-089-X
ISBN 13: 978-1-58159-089-0
© 2000 Handyman Club of America
7 8 9 / 15 14 13 12 11 10

Handyman Club of America
12301 Whitewater Drive
Minnetonka, Minnesota 55343
www.handymanclub.com

Contents

Firewood Box (12)

Building Blocks (66)

Heavy-duty Sandbox (98)

Patio Tea Table (24)

Five-board Bench (8)

Recipe Holder (126)

Kid-size Picnic Table (38)

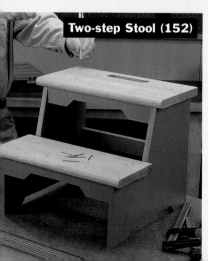
Two-step Stool (152)

Funtime Toy Box (112)

Tool Tote (44)

Entry Bench (70)

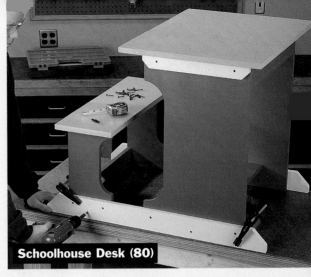
Schoolhouse Desk (80)

Full-shelter Doghouse (138)

Easy-clean Birdhouse (102)

Garden Bench (144)

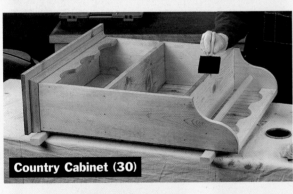
Country Cabinet (30)

Wall-hung Coatrack (74)

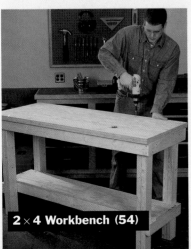
2 × 4 Workbench (54)

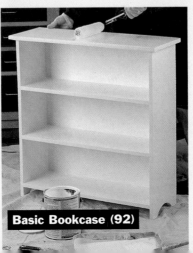
Basic Bookcase (92)

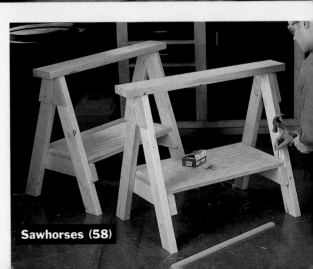
Sawhorses (58)

Introduction

If weekends and evenings are the only times you have for woodworking, this book was written for you. *Quick & Easy Woodworking Projects,* published exclusively for Handyman Club of America Members, contains a roster of 28 attractive projects you can build from start to finish in a day or less.

Maybe making sawdust is a new hobby and you're still mastering the basics—measuring, cutting, drilling, routing and assembly. Great! We've designed these projects with you in mind as well. Regardless of what order you build these projects, you'll discover good opportunities for honing your skills. Better yet, the materials cost for these projects is modest so learning the ropes won't break your budget.

We at the Handyman Club believe that woodworking is a pastime that can be enjoyed by everyone—whether you've spent the better part of your life cutting wood or you're just starting out. To this end, each of the projects in this book is presented with a complete cutting and shopping list, detailed drawings, full-color photographs of the project as it's being built and straightforward step-by-step instructions to help you every step of the way.

Before you get started, review this page and the next for more information about gathering the power tools you'll need and some helpful advice concerning driving screws and making patterns.

TOOLS YOU'LL NEED

The television version of woodworking these days may lead you to believe that the best way to build something respectable is to spend a fortune on tools. This book will prove that such a notion is simply untrue. In fact, most if not all of the power tools you'll need for building these projects may be in your toolbox already. If you own a circular saw (A) or jig saw (B), drill/driver (C) and sander (D), you've got all the woodworking tools required to build most of these projects. Borrow or buy a router (E) and you'll be able to build the rest.

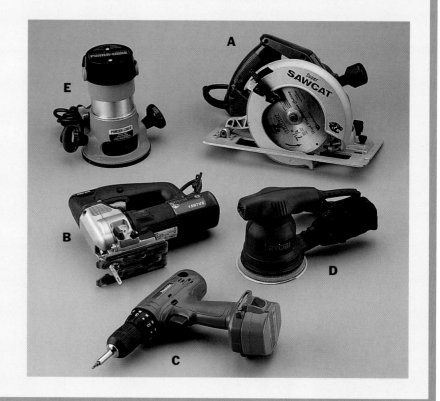

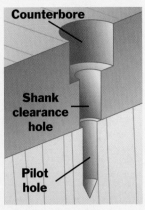

Counterbore

Shank clearance hole

Pilot hole

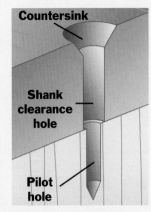

Countersink

Shank clearance hole

Pilot hole

A counterbore bit can drill a pilot hole, screw shank hole and counterbore hole all at the same time. The counterbore is sized to fit a wood plug, which conceals the screwhead.

A countersink bit reams out the top of a pilot hole with a bevel so the screwhead can be driven slightly below the surface. This creates a shallow recess that can be filled with wood putty.

COUNTERSINKING VS. COUNTERBORING SCREWS

Screws are popular fasteners for reinforcing wood joints, and you'll find them used often in this book. Depending on the project, you'll need to recess the screwheads or, in some cases conceal them altogether. Two methods for doing this are counterboring and countersinking. Counterboring involves drilling a pilot hole for the screw as well as a larger hole for driving the screwhead entirely below the surface. The counterbore is sized to fit a wood plug, which hides the screw. Countersinking is simply reaming the surface of the pilot hole so the screwhead sits flush or just below the wood surface. Counterboring and countersinking bits are inexpensive and worth adding to your bit collection.

MAKING & USING PATTERNS

When building from published plans, you may need to create a full-size pattern to duplicate curved or irregular shapes from technical drawings onto your project parts. One option is to make a full-size template from scrap, like hardboard, then trace the template shape onto workpieces. Templates are especially worth the effort if you plan to build the project again. Otherwise, you can draw a grid directly on the workpiece at full size. Then use the grid drawing in the printed plans as a square-by-square reference for plotting and transferring the shape onto the workpiece.

Make a template

Draw or photocopy then transfer the full-size shape onto template material (hardboard is shown here), and cut out the template with a jig saw or coping saw. Smooth the template edges. Trace its shape onto your workpiece. Save the template for reuse.

Follow a grid drawing

Draw a scaled grid on your workpiece, then re-create the pattern by plotting points onto your grid using the printed pattern as a reference. Connect the points with a solid line to draw the shape. You may find it helpful to use a compass or flexible ruler to draw curves.

Five-board Bench

Bring a classic piece of Colonial Americana into your home when you build this five-board bench project. True to its name, this bench consists of only five parts that you can cut and assemble in just a few hours. Our design seats two adults or three children comfortably.

Vital statistics

TYPE: Five-board bench

OVERALL SIZE: 48L by 18H by 11¼D

MATERIAL: Pine

JOINERY: Butt joints reinforced with glue and screws

CONSTRUCTION DETAILS:
· Stretchers recess into notches cut in legs
· Matching pairs of stretchers and legs allow for gang-cutting parts to speed construction

FINISH: Primer and paint

BUILDING TIME: 2-3 hours

Shopping List

- ☐ (1) 1 × 12 in. × 8 ft. pine
- ☐ (1) 1 × 12 in. × 4 ft. pine
- ☐ #8 × 2-in. flathead wood screws
- ☐ ⅜-in.-dia. wood plugs (optional)
- ☐ Wood glue
- ☐ Finishing materials

Five-board Bench: Step-by-step

LAY OUT THE PARTS

❶ Measure and cut workpieces for making the legs and stretchers: Cut a 35-in. length of the long pine board for the legs and a 47-in.-long piece for the stretchers. Rip the leg piece to 10¼ in. wide and crosscut into two 17¼-in. lengths. Rip the two 4½-in.-wide stretchers from the 47-in. workpiece.

❷ Lay out the legs: First, measure and mark the two ¾-in.-deep, 4½-in.-long stretcher notches along the top outside edges of each leg. Then draw the V-shaped cutout on the bottom of each leg to form the bench feet. Start the V-shape 3 in. up from the bottom of the legs, centered on the width of each leg. Make reference marks 2½ in. in from the edges of the legs along the bottom to mark for the bench feet. Connect the V-cutout reference marks with a straightedge **(See Photo A).**

❸ Draw the tapered ends on the stretchers. Refer to the *Stretcher End Layout,* page 10, to measure and mark your cutting lines.

CUT THE PARTS

❹ Trim the ends of each stretcher with a jig saw to form the tapers on the ends of these parts.

PHOTO A: Lay out the stretcher notches as well as the V-shaped leg cutouts with a straightedge.

❺ Cut the legs to shape. You could cut out the leg details one leg at a time, but most jig saw blades are long enough to allow you to gang-cut both legs at once. To do this, stack the legs on top of one another and in the same orientation. Clamp the assembly to your bench so the stretcher notch areas overhang the bench. Cut along your layout lines to form the two stretcher notches in both legs. Cut slowly and carefully to keep the jig saw blade from bending and veering off course as you cut. Once the stretcher notches are cut, unclamp the legs, turn them around on the bench so the V-notch areas overhang, reclamp and make the remaining cuts **(See Photo B).**

Five-board Bench

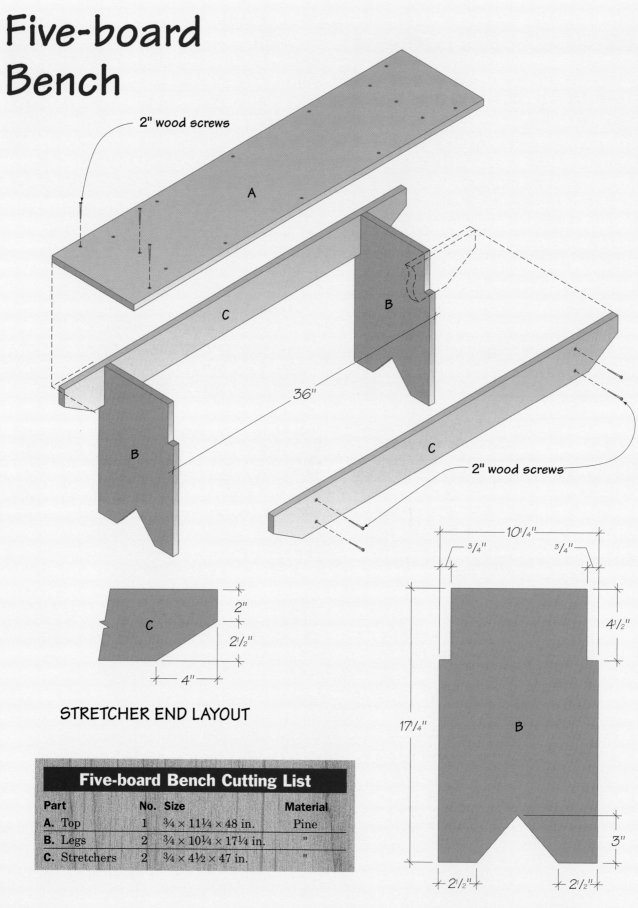

2" wood screws

A

C

B

B

36"

C

2" wood screws

2"
2½"
C
4"

STRETCHER END LAYOUT

10¼"
¾"   ¾"
4½"
17¼"
B
3"
2½"   2½"

LEG LAYOUT

Five-board Bench Cutting List			
Part	**No.**	**Size**	**Material**
A. Top	1	¾ × 11¼ × 48 in.	Pine
B. Legs	2	¾ × 10¼ × 17¼ in.	"
C. Stretchers	2	¾ × 4½ × 47 in.	"

ASSEMBLE THE BENCH

6 Attach the stretchers to the legs: Draw a reference line across the width of each stretcher, 5⅞ in. from the ends to mark the leg locations. Spread glue in the stretcher notches on the legs. Clamp the legs in place between the stretchers so the legs are centered on the stretcher reference lines you just drew. Drill pairs of countersunk pilot holes through the stretchers and into the legs, and fasten the parts with #8 × 2-in. flat-head wood screws.

7 Install the bench top: Lay the bench top on the stretcher/leg assembly so it overhangs evenly all around, and mark this position on the bottom face of the bench top. (If you've measured and cut accurately, the overhang should be ½ in.) Remove the bench top, spread glue along the top edges of the stretchers and clamp the bench top in position. Attach the top by driving countersunk screws into the legs and stretchers (three screws per leg and five screws per stretcher, spaced evenly) **(See Photo C).**

FINISHING TOUCHES

8 Fill the holes left by the screwheads. Since we painted our bench, we used wood putty to conceal the screws. You could also install wood plugs, which look more natural on a bench that will be stained and/or varnished.

9 Sand all surfaces of the bench smooth with up to 150-grit sandpaper. Apply your topcoat of choice. We brushed on a coat of primer followed by several coats of paint.

PHOTO B: Clamp the leg blanks one on top of the other so you can cut them both at once with a jig saw.

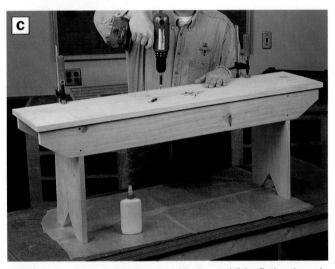

PHOTO C: Assemble the bench parts with glue and 2-in. flathead wood screws, driven into countersunk pilot holes.

Five-board benches

Five-board benches have been an American furniture mainstay since Colonial times. Their utilitarian styling and simple construction have made them common fixtures in barns, workshops and even around long dinner tables. You'll find five-board benches made of just about any available wood and in all lengths and heights, but usually they're constructed from pine and painted. The splayed legs typically are scalloped or notched to create feet. Many shorter benches also have handle cutouts in the top. If you decide to build a five-board bench for outdoor use, it's a good idea to construct it from a naturally weather-resistant wood like cedar or white oak instead of pine.

Firewood Box

Y̲ou'll always be ready to prepare a cozy fire if you store your
firewood next to the hearth in this rustic firewood box. Made
of cedar, our design features a covered bin for storing the firewood
and a narrower compartment for kindling.

Vital statistics

TYPE: Firewood box

OVERALL SIZE: 28L by 23¼H by 20⅜D

MATERIAL: Cedar

JOINERY: Butt joints reinforced with screws

CONSTRUCTION DETAILS:
- All parts crosscut from dimensional 1 × 4 cedar
- Sides and divider are assembled into panels before the angled top profiles are cut

FINISH: Clear deck sealer or none

BUILDING TIME: 4-5 hours

Shopping List

☐ (10) 1 × 4 in. × 10 ft. cedar

☐ (2) 3-in. galvanized butt hinges

☐ Deck screws (1¼-, 2-in.)

☐ 12-in. length of ½-in.-dia. braided nylon rope

Firewood Box: Step-by-step

MAKE THE BOTTOM, SIDES, DIVIDER & FRONT PANEL

❶ Crosscut the bottom, side/divider and front slats to length.

❷ Cut the six side corner boards (both front and rear) as well as the front corner boards and skids to length.

❸ Assemble the sides. Despite the fact that the sides eventually will be trimmed at an angle from front to back, build them as rectangular panels first, with six slats and a front and rear-side corner board. Arrange the parts so the rear-side corner board is flush with the back ends of the slats and the front edge of the front-side corner board extends ⅞ in. beyond the

PHOTO A: Assemble the bottom, sides, divider and front panel. Join the slats to corner boards or skids with 1¼-in. deck screws. You may find it helpful to clamp the slats together to keep them aligned when driving the screws.

front ends of the slats. Secure the parts with counter-sunk 1¼-in. deck screws, driving the screws through the slats and into the corner boards.

❹ Build the divider: Join six divider slats to the front and rear-side corner boards with 1¼-in. deck

Firewood Box

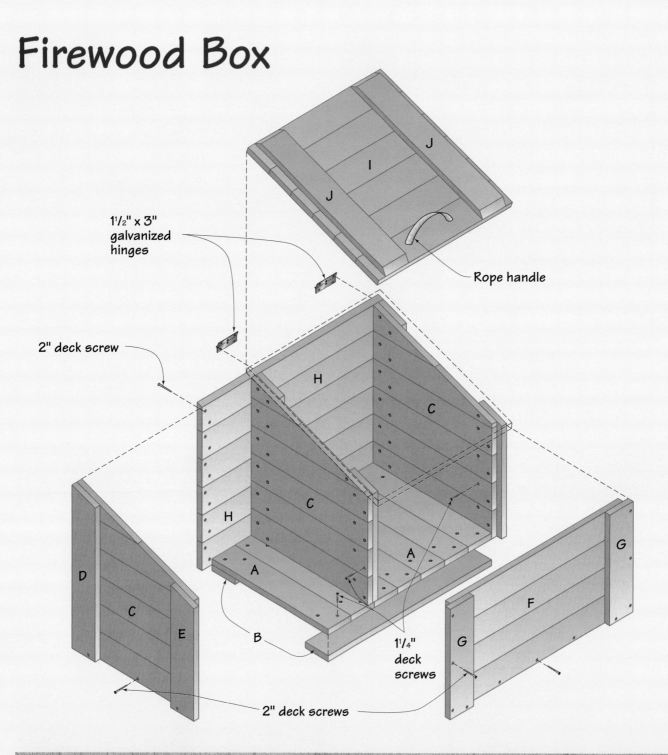

1½" x 3" galvanized hinges

2" deck screw

Rope handle

I

J

J

J

H

C

C

H

C

A

D

C

E

B

A

F

G

G

1¼" deck screws

2" deck screws

Firewood Box Cutting List

Part	No.	Size	Material	Part	No.	Size	Material
A. Bottom slats	7	$\frac{7}{8} \times 3\frac{1}{2} \times 17\frac{3}{4}$ in.	Cedar	**F.** Front slats	4	$\frac{7}{8} \times 3\frac{1}{2} \times 26\frac{1}{4}$ in.	Cedar
B. Skids	2	$\frac{7}{8} \times 3\frac{1}{2} \times 24\frac{1}{2}$ in.	"	**G.** Front corner boards	2	$\frac{7}{8} \times 3\frac{1}{2} \times 14$ in.	"
C. Side/divider slats	18	$\frac{7}{8} \times 3\frac{1}{2} \times 17\frac{3}{4}$ in.	"	**H.** Back slats	6	$\frac{7}{8} \times 3\frac{1}{2} \times 28$ in.	"
D. Side corner boards (rear)	3	$\frac{7}{8} \times 3\frac{1}{2} \times 21$ in.	"	**I.** Lid slats	6	$\frac{7}{8} \times 3\frac{1}{2} \times 20\frac{1}{4}$ in.	"
E. Side corner boards (front)	3	$\frac{7}{8} \times 3\frac{1}{2} \times 16$ in.	"	**J.** Lid battens	2	$\frac{7}{8} \times 3\frac{1}{2} \times 21$ in.	

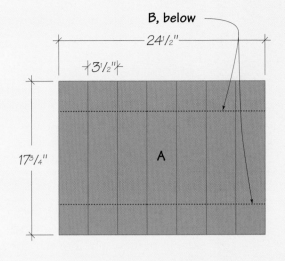

BOTTOM - SLAT LAYOUT

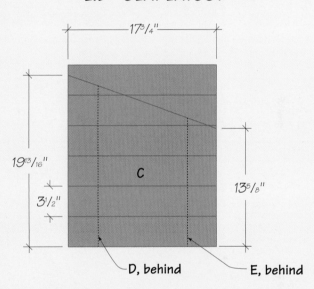

LID - SLAT LAYOUT

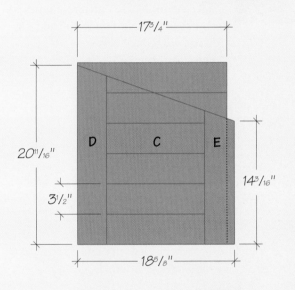

SIDE - SLAT LAYOUT

INTERIOR DIVIDER - SLAT LAYOUT

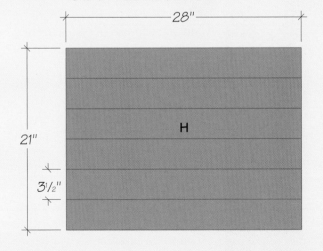

BACK - SLAT LAYOUT

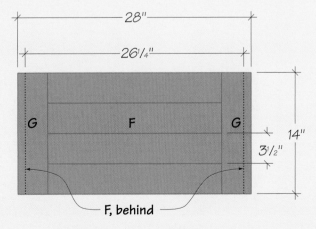

FRONT - SLAT LAYOUT

PHOTO B: Mark the side panels and divider with a cutting line for the top angled profile, then clamp a straightedge to guide your saw and cut the side panels to shape.

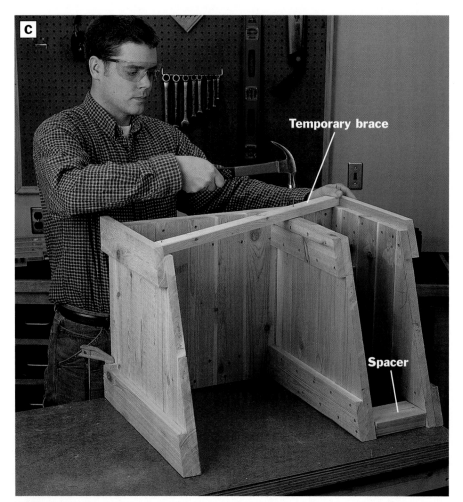

PHOTO C: Hold the partially assembled firewood box square by tacking a temporary brace diagonally across the front of the project. Insert and tack a 6-in. spacer between the divider and the closer side as well.

screws. The outside edges of the corner boards should align with the ends of the slats.

❺ Make the front: Arrange the front slats and front corner boards so the outside edges of the corner boards extend 7/8 in. beyond the ends of the slats on both sides. These corner boards will overlap the front corner boards on the side panels when the project is assembled. Screw the parts together, driving the deck screws through the front slats and into the front corner boards.

❻ Assemble the bottom: Fasten the seven bottom slats to the two skids with deck screws so the slats are flush with the ends and outside edges of the skids (**See Photo A**).

❼ Trim the sides and divider to shape: Lay out the angled profile that forms the shape of the top of each side and the divider, according to the slat layout drawings for these parts, found on page 15. Cut the angles with a circular saw or jig saw guided against a straightedge (**See Photo B**).

BUILD THE FIREWOOD BOX
❽ Assemble the sides, divider and bottom: Clamp the sides to the bottom so the bottom edge of each side is flush with the bottom of each skid. Drive 2-in. deck screws through the sides and into the bottom. Install the divider so the divider slats are spaced 6 in. from the slats of one of the sides. Drive 2-in. deck screws up through the bottom and into the divider to attach the parts. Hold the sides and divider square to the bottom by nailing a temporary brace diagonally across the front of the project to the sides and divider. Tack a 6-in.-long spacer between the

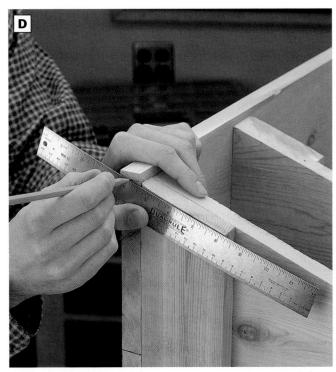

PHOTO D: After you've installed the first five back slats with screws, set the top back slat in place and mark the angle formed by the sides onto the back slat with a straightedge.

PHOTO E: Bevel-rip the top back slat along its full length with the saw set to the angle you marked in Step 11. Since the slat is narrow and the cut is right along the board's edge, hold it steady by tacking the slat to a couple of scraps, and clamp the scraps to your workbench. You may also need to clamp a board of the same thickness as the slat next to the slat to provide more support for the saw base. Be sure to allow an inch or so of space between this board and the slat to provide clear space for the strip of wood you are cutting free.

divider and closer side as well (**See Photo C**).

INSTALL THE BACK & FRONT

9 Cut the six back slats to length.

10 Attach five back slats to the firewood box assembly: Starting from the bottom of the project and working up, drive pairs of 2-in. deck screws through each back slat and into the sides. Offset the screw pattern. The bottom slat should be flush with the bottoms of the skids. Drive a single screw through each slat and into the divider.

11 Set the top back slat in place and mark the angles of the sides onto the slat ends (**See Photo D**).

12 Bevel-cut the top edge of the top back slat. We nailed the slat temporarily to a couple of scraps clamped to the workbench to hold the clamp securely while making the cut (**See Photo E**).

PHOTO F: Position the top back slat so its beveled edge matches the angles of the sides, and secure the slat to the firewood box with 2-in. deck screws.

PHOTO G: Remove the temporary brace and install the front panel with screws. Drive countersunk deck screws through the front corner boards into the sides as well as through the bottom slat into the firewood box bottom.

PHOTO H: Clamp the six lid slats together so their ends align. Position the lid battens beneath the slat assembly, inset 1 in. from the ends of the slats. Fasten the parts with countersunk 1¼-in. deck screws driven down through the slats and into the battens.

13 Attach the top back slat to the sides and divider with 2-in. deck screws **(See Photo F).**

14 Remove the temporary brace and spacer.

15 Set the front panel onto the front of the project so the bottom of the panel is flush with the bottom of the front skid. Fasten the front to the side slats, divider and bottom with 2-in. deck screws **(See Photo G).**

16 Bevel the top ends of the front corner boards to match the slope of the sides: Use a rasp, block plane or coarse file to shave down the front corner boards. Doing so will allow the lid to close fully over the firewood compartment.

BUILD THE LID
17 Crosscut the eight lid slats and two lid battens to length.

18 Arrange the lid slats on the battens so the ends of the slats are aligned and the battens are inset 1 in. from the slat ends. Hold the slats together with clamps. Drive 1¼-in. deck screws through the slats and into the battens. Stagger the screw pattern, installing a pair of screws at each batten location on the slats **(See Photo H).**

FINISHING TOUCHES
19 Sand the project smooth and ease the edges and corners to keep the cedar from splintering.

20 Apply your choice of finish. We topcoated all surfaces of the project with two coats of clear deck sealer to preserve the rich cedar wood tone **(See Photo I).** You could also leave the project unfinished, but the cedar eventually will turn a gray color if exposed to direct sunlight or moisture. Cedar also takes wood stain well, if you wish to match the project to other woodwork in the room.

㉑ Fashion a rope pull for the lid: Drill a pair of ½-in.-dia. holes about 6 in. apart through the front lid slat. Thread a length of ½-in.-dia. braided rope down through these holes in the lid, and knot the ends of the rope to form a lid pull.

㉒ Attach the lid: Set the lid in place over the firewood compartment so the ends of the lid are flush with a side, the divider and the back slats. Lay out locations on the lid and top back slat for a pair of hinges. We positioned the hinges even with the lid battens, with the hinge knuckles facing outward. Drill pilot holes for the hinge screws, and screw the hinges in place (See Photo J).

PHOTO I (Optional): Topcoat the project with clear or tinted deck sealer. Brush on a coat of wood stain, if you prefer. It isn't necessary to apply finish to the project if it will be located inside and out of direct sunlight. Finish will enhance the wood tones and grain.

PHOTO J: Attach the lid to the project with a couple of 3-in. galvanized butt hinges. Position the lid so it covers the firewood compartment but not the kindling compartment.

Desktop Book Rack

Need a gift idea for a college student you know? You'll be the wise gift giver when you present this Arts-and-Crafts inspired desktop book rack. Made of red oak and decorated with authentic wedge-pinned through tenons, this useful project takes up little more desktop than a legal notepad and keeps important books within arm's reach.

Desktop Book Rack: Step-by-step

MAKE THE SIDES, BACK & SHELF

1 Crosscut workpieces for the sides, back and shelf, sized according to the *Cutting List,* page 22.

2 Lay out and cut the sides to shape: Make a full-size paper grid drawing of the sides, according to the *Side Layout* drawing, page 22. Cut out the paper shape and use it as a template for drawing the sides onto the side workpieces. Cut out the sides with a jig saw.

3 Rip-cut the back and shelf to

PHOTO A: Lay out and cut the two sides, back and shelf pieces to shape. Since the back and shelf parts are identical, clamp them together and gang-cut both with a jig saw.

width. Mark and cut the through tenons on the ends of the back and shelf pieces. Refer to the *Tenon Layout* drawing, page 22, to mark

the shape of the tenons and wedge holes on the ends of the back and shelves. Cut the through tenons to shape **(See Photo A).**

Desktop Book Rack

TENON LAYOUT

WEDGE LAYOUT

1" squares

SIDE LAYOUT

Desktop Book Rack Cutting List			
Part	No.	Size	Material
A. Sides	2	¾ × 7½ × 9½ in.	Red oak
B. Back/shelf	2	½ × 3½ × 19 in.	"
C. Wedges	4	½ × 9⁄16 × 1¼ in.	"

PHOTO B: Drill out the centers of the wedge holes in the tenons with a ½-in. bit. Use the same bit for boring holes in the ends of the mortises in the sides. If you align the parts carefully and clamp them together, it's possible to drill through both parts at once.

PHOTO C: Clean out the remaining waste from the mortises in the sides with a jig saw. Square up the wedge holes and the ends of the mortises with a sharp chisel and a file.

PHOTO D: Lay out and cut four tenon wedges from ½-in.-thick stock. Cut the wedges a little wider than necessary so you can sand them as needed for a good fit in the wedge holes.

PHOTO E: Assemble the sides, back and shelf with clamps, then glue and insert the wedges into the wedge holes. Tap the wedges snug with a wood mallet. Wipe away excess glue before it dries.

CUT THE WEDGE HOLES & MORTISES

❹ Drill out the waste from the four tenon wedge holes with a sharp ½-in.-dia. brad point bit.

❺ Cut out the mortises in the sides for the back and shelf tenons. First bore ½-in.-dia holes at the ends of each mortise (**See Photo B**). Then saw out the rest of the waste in between the holes. Square up the wedge holes and the mortises with a sharp ½-in. chisel, then clean up the cutouts with a narrow file (**See Photo C**).

ASSEMBLE & FINISH THE BOOK RACK

❻ Make the wedges: Refer to the *Wedge Layout* drawing, page 22, for marking the wedge shapes on a strip of ½-in.-thick stock. NOTE: *Lay out the wedges so the grain runs lengthwise.* Cut out the wedges with a jig saw so they are slightly wider than your layout lines (**See Photo D**).

❼ Dry-fit the book rack together. The tenons should seat fully into the mortises when you interlock the parts. Adjust the fit of the mortises and tenons by sanding the tenons a little at a time. Aim for a snug, but not forced, fit of the tenons in the mortises.

❽ Dry-fit the wedges into their holes in the tenons with the angled edges of the wedges facing the book rack sides. The wedges should overhang the tenons evenly when fully inserted. Sand the wedges until they fit properly.

❾ Disassemble the book rack and sand all the parts smooth. Reassemble, this time gluing the wedges into the tenons (**See Photo E**). Wipe off excess glue immediately with a damp rag.

❿ Wipe or brush on your choice of stain, followed by a clear topcoat. We wiped on two coats of Danish oil.

Patio Tea Table

Whether you're enjoying coffee and the morning paper or a cool afternoon beverage, spend more of your leisure time outside with the help of this attractive patio table. You'll find many uses for its spacious top and lower shelf: from serving a crew of thirsty kids to hosting a casual game of cards. Our table is made of cedar, an inexpensive wood that is naturally weather resistant and easy to work with.

Vital statistics

TYPE: Patio table

OVERALL SIZE: 29½ dia. by 18⅞H

MATERIAL: Cedar

JOINERY: Butt joints reinforced with screws

CONSTRUCTION DETAILS:
· Round top cut to shape with a jig saw guided by a shop-made circle-cutting jig
· Both shelf and top slats held apart with spacers during installation to promote water drainage

FINISH: Clear deck sealer or none

BUILDING TIME: 6-8 hours

Shopping List

☐ (3) 1 × 4 in. × 8 ft. cedar
☐ (2) 2 × 2 in. × 8 ft. cedar
☐ Deck screws (1½-, 2½-in.)
☐ Finishing materials

Patio Tea Table: Step-by-step

ASSEMBLE THE SHELF

1 Crosscut the shelf frame pieces and four slats to length, according to the *Cutting List,* page 26.

2 Assemble the shelf frame: Arrange the frame pieces so that one pair overlaps the ends of the other pair. Clamp the frame members in place, using clamp pads to keep from marring the soft cedar. Drill one pilot hole at each corner and attach the frame pieces to one another with 2½-in. deck screws **(See Photo A).**

PHOTO A: Clamp the four shelf frame members together so the ends of one pair overlap the ends of the other pair, then attach the frame parts with a single deck screw at each joint. Insert clamp pads between the clamp jaws and the frame to keep from marring the soft cedar.

Patio Tea Table

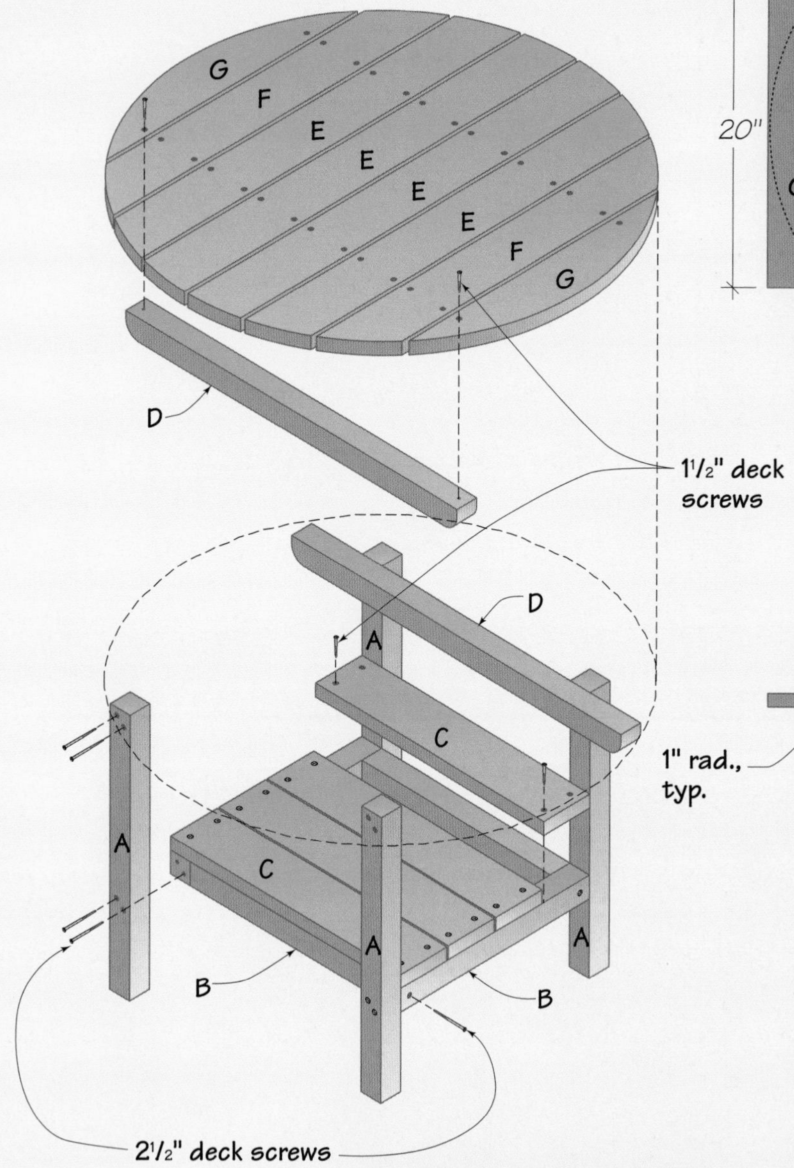
G
F
E
E
E
E
F
G
D
1½" deck screws
D
A
C
A
C
A
A
B
B
2½" deck screws

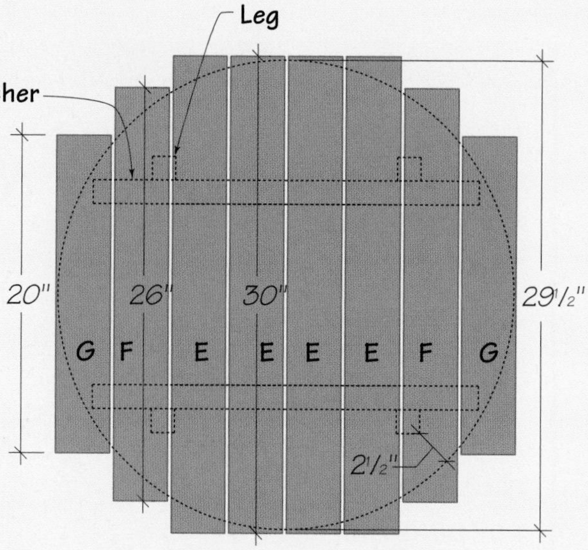
Leg
Top stretcher
20"
26"
30"
29½"
G F E E E E F G
2½"

TOP SLATS LAYOUT

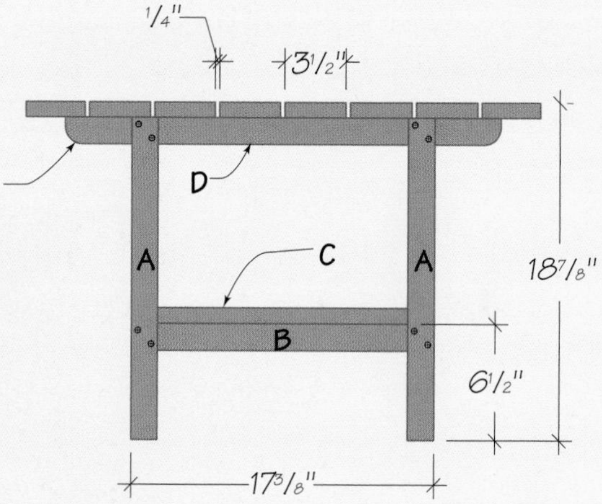
¼"
3½"
1" rad., typ.
D
A
C
A
B
18⅞"
6½"
17⅜"

ELEVATION

Patio Tea Table Cutting List

Part	No.	Size	Material
A. Legs	4	1½ × 1½ × 18 in.	Cedar
B. Shelf frames	4	1½ × 1½ × 14⅜ in.	"
C. Shelf slats	4	⅞ × 4 × 17⅜ in.	"
D. Stretchers	2	1½ × 1½ × 25 in.	"
E. Top slats (long)	4	⅞ × 4 × 30 in.	"
F. Top slats (medium)	2	⅞ × 4 × 26 in.	"
G. Top slats (short)	2	⅞ × 4 × 20 in.	"

3 Attach the shelf slats. Begin by placing one slat so it is flush with one long side of the frame. Attach this slat with four countersunk 1½-in. deck screws. Then lay out the remaining three slats on the frame so the fourth slat is flush with the opposite side of the shelf frame. Adjust the two middle slats so there is an even spacing between all of the slats (about ¼ in., although this spacing may vary, depending on the actual width of the cedar stock you buy). Locate a pair of scrap spacers that match the slat spacing width you've determined. Then drill pilot holes and install the remaining slats, one at a time, with the spacers inserted **(See Photo B).**

MAKE THE LEG ASSEMBLIES

4 Crosscut the legs and stretchers to length, then scribe a 1-in. radius on both ends of the two stretchers with a compass.

5 Round over the stretcher ends with a jig saw **(See Photo C).**

6 Attach the legs to the stretchers: Position a pair of legs on each stretcher so the top ends of the legs are flush with the top (flat) edge of the stretchers. NOTE: *The rounded corners of the stretchers should face the bottoms of the legs.* Inset the legs 3¾ in. from the ends of each stretcher. Drill two pilot holes through each leg into the stretcher, and attach the parts with 2½-in. deck screws **(See Photo D).**

JOIN THE SHELF TO THE LEG ASSEMBLIES

7 Fasten the leg assemblies to the shelf: First cut four 5-in.-long 2 × 4 scrap blocks to support the shelf when joining it to the leg assemblies. Set the shelf on top of the scrap blocks set on end. Posi-

PHOTO B: Attach one slat flush to one long side of the shelf frame. Position the remaining slats evenly across the frame with temporary spacers inserted in between. The ends and edges of the slats should not overlap the frame.

PHOTO C: Mark the bottom corners of the stretchers with a 1-in.-radius curve, then trim the corners to shape with a jig saw. Be sure to secure the workpiece with clamps before you cut.

tion the leg assemblies, one on each long side of the shelf, so the stretchers face inward and the outside edges of the legs are flush with the ends of the shelf frame. Drive two countersunk 2½-in. deck screws through each leg and into the shelf frame (**See Photo E**). Position the screws carefully so they do not hit the shelf frame assembly screws.

INSTALL & SHAPE THE TOP

8 Lay out and attach the top slats to the stretchers. Be aware that the slats vary in length according to their position on the table. Position the two shortest slats at the ends of the stretchers, followed by the medium slats. The four long slats make up the middle of the table. The space between the two long center slats should mark the center of the stretchers. Insert spacer scraps between the

PHOTO D: Fasten the legs to the stretchers so the top ends of the legs align with the top (flat) edges of the stretchers. Scrap 2 × 4 spacers provide level support for the legs while you attach them to the stretchers with countersunk screws.

PHOTO E: Elevate the shelf to its proper height in relation to the legs with four 5-in.-long 2 × 4 scraps. Position a leg assembly against each long edge of the shelf, with the stretchers facing inward. Drill offset pilot holes through the legs, and secure the legs to the shelf frame with 2½-in. deck screws.

PHOTO F: Arrange and fasten the top slats across the stretchers. The shortest slats should overhang the ends of the stretchers, followed by the medium and long slats. Hold the slats evenly apart with scrap spacers. Work outward from the center to the ends, inserting spacers as you go, and fasten the slats with countersunk 1½-in. deck screws.

slats to keep them separated evenly. Attach the slats to the stretchers with 1½-in. deck screws, driving two screws per joint **(See Photo F)**.

9 Cut the tabletop to shape with a jig saw: We used a simple circle-cutting jig, which consists of a 3-ft. strip of plywood outfitted on one end with a frame to hold the jig saw base. A hole cut in the blade area inside the frame provides clearance for the blade. The jig pivots around a nail tacked at the center of the circle. The distance from the blade to the nail establishes the circle's radius. If you choose to use this jig rather than cut freehand, locate the tabletop centerpoint to determine the position of the jig's pivot nail. Since the center of this tabletop lands on a space between two slats, tack a scrap piece of thin material (we used a piece of ⅛-in.-thick hardboard) to the tabletop to provide a nailing surface for the pivot nail. Set the distance from the pivot point to the blade to 14¾ in. and tack the pivot nail into place. It's a good idea to insert a pencil into the blade hole and lay out the full circumference of the circle before starting to cut; this way you can monitor how the blade tracks the layout line as you cut. Then insert the saw in the jig and trim the top to shape, starting as close as possible to the edge of one of the short top slats **(See Photo G)**.

FINISHING TOUCHES

10 Give the project a thorough sanding, particularly around the curved edge of the table to ease all sharp edges and corners.

11 Topcoat the project with several coats of clear deck sealer, if you wish, to help preserve the cedar wood tones **(See Photo H)**.

PHOTO G: A circle-cutting jig saw jig makes easy, accurate work of cutting the tabletop to shape. Since the middle of the circle falls between slats, you'll need to tack a thin scrap to the tabletop to provide a stable anchor for the pivot nail. Use the jig to mark a cutting line with a pencil first. Then insert the saw and pivot the jig around the nail to cut the tabletop to shape.

PHOTO H: Sand the project to remove splinters and to break the edges. Then brush on several coats of clear deck sealer to help protect the wood from the elements.

Country Cabinet

Here's an attractive kitchen accent piece that includes a convenient towel rack. Built from pine and beadboard plywood, this cabinet conjures up images of country stores and farm kitchens of yesteryear. Finally, a place to display that art glass or cookie jar collection!

Vital statistics

TYPE: Wall-mounted open cabinet

OVERALL SIZE: 32L by 29W by 9¼D

MATERIAL: Pine, beadboard plywood

JOINERY: Butt joints reinforced with glue and nails

CONSTRUCTION DETAILS:
· Cove molding miter-cut to fit around cabinet top
· Towel rod secured with a finish nail on each end

FINISH: Stain, varnish

BUILDING TIME: 4-5 hours

Shopping List

☐ (1) 1 × 4 in. × 6 ft. pine

☐ (1) 1 × 8 in. × 10 ft. pine

☐ (1) 1 × 10 in. × 4 ft. pine

☐ (1) ¾ × 1⅛ in. × 4 ft. pine cove molding

☐ (1) 1-in.-dia. × 2-ft. dowel

☐ (1) ¼ in. × 4 ft. × 4 ft. pine beadboard plywood

☐ ¾-in. brads

☐ Finish nails (1½-, 2-in.)

☐ Wood glue

☐ Finishing materials

Country Cabinet: Step-by-step

MAKE THE SIDES, APRON & BOTTOM TRIM

❶ Crosscut two 31¼-in. boards for the cabinet sides.

❷ Crosscut two 24-in. lengths from the pine 1 × 4 to make the apron and bottom trim. Rip-cut the bottom trim piece to a width of 2½ in.

❸ Draw the curved profiles on the cabinet sides: Make a full-size paper template of the curved profile shown on the *Side Section* drawing, page 33. Position the

PHOTO A: Create a full-size paper template to draw the curved profiles on the bottoms of the cabinet side panels. Tape the template to each side workpiece and draw the curves.

Country Cabinet

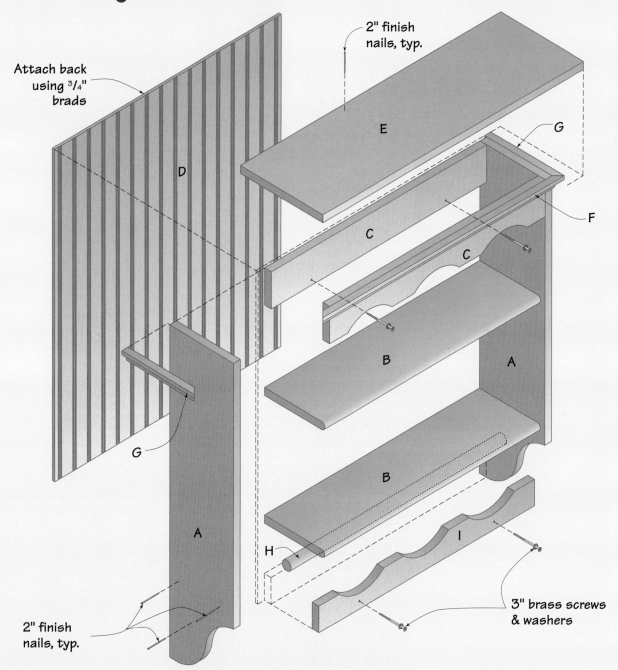

Attach back using ³/₄" brads

2" finish nails, typ.

2" finish nails, typ.

3" brass screws & washers

A
B
C
D
E
F
G
H
I

Country Cabinet Cutting List

Part	No.	Size	Material
A. Sides	2	³/₄ × 7¼ × 31¼ in.	Pine
B. Shelf	2	³/₄ × 7¼ × 24 in.	"
C. Nailer/apron	2	³/₄ × 3½ × 24 in.	"
D. Back	1	¼ × 25½ × 31¼ in.	Beadboard plywood
E. Top	1	³/₄ × 9¼ × 29 in.	Pine

Part	No.	Size	Material
F. Front molding	1	³/₄ × 1⅛ × 27 in.	Pine cove molding
G. Side molding	2	³/₄ × 1⅛ × 8¼ in.	"
H. Towel rod	1	1 in. dia. × 24 in.	Dowel
I. Bottom trim	1	³/₄ × 2½ × 24 in.	Pine

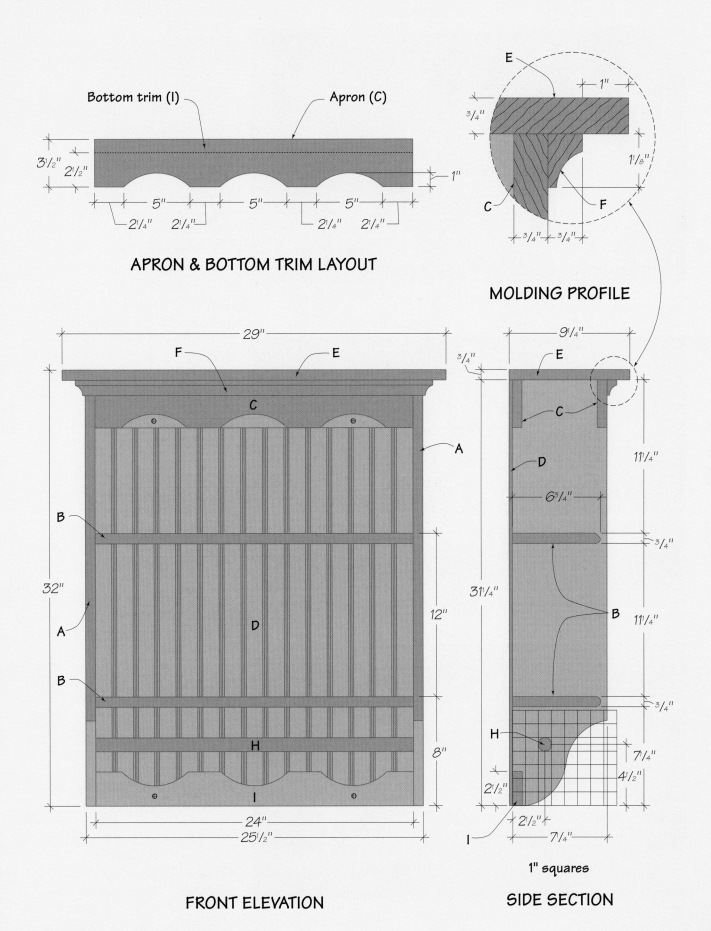

Bottom trim (I)

Apron (C)

$3\frac{1}{2}''$ $2\frac{1}{2}''$

$5''$ $5''$ $5''$

$2\frac{1}{4}''$ $2\frac{1}{4}''$ $2\frac{1}{4}''$ $2\frac{1}{4}''$

$1''$

APRON & BOTTOM TRIM LAYOUT

E

$1''$

$3/4''$

$1\frac{1}{8}''$

C

$3/4''$ $3/4''$

F

MOLDING PROFILE

F

E

$29''$

C

A

B

$32''$

A

D

$12''$

B

H

$8''$

I

$24''$

$25\frac{1}{2}''$

FRONT ELEVATION

$3/4''$

$9\frac{1}{4}''$

E

C

D

$11\frac{1}{4}''$

$6\frac{3}{4}''$

$3/4''$

$31\frac{1}{4}''$

B

$11\frac{1}{4}''$

$3/4''$

H

$7\frac{1}{4}''$

$4\frac{1}{2}''$

$2\frac{1}{2}''$

$2\frac{1}{2}''$

$7\frac{1}{4}''$

I

1" squares

SIDE SECTION

PHOTO B: Lay out the arches on the apron and bottom trim pieces. A one-gallon paint can serves as a good template to draw the curves.

PHOTO C: Cut the curved profiles in the sides, apron and bottom trim pieces with a jig saw.

PHOTO D: Glue and clamp the top and bottom shelves to one of the cabinet sides. Reinforce the joints with 2-in. finish nails.

template on each side panel, and draw the curves (See Photo A).

❹ Lay out the arches on the apron and bottom trim pieces: See the *Apron & Bottom Trim Layout* drawing, page 33, for marking the three arch positions on both parts. You could use a compass to draw the curves, but we found that a gallon-size paint can makes an easy template. Set the can in position on your layout marks, and draw the curves (See Photo B).

❺ Cut the curved profiles in the sides, apron and bottom trim pieces with a jig saw. Clamp each part to your worksurface to hold it steady while you make the cuts (See Photo C).

❻ Smooth the curved cuts and remove any saw marks with a file.

❼ Sand the sides, apron and bottom trim workpieces smooth with 150-grit sandpaper. It's easier to sand these parts now while all surfaces are accessible than after you begin assembly.

MAKE THE SHELVES, NAILER & TOP

❽ Lay out and crosscut two 24-in. shelves from pine 1 × 8.

❾ Cut the cabinet top to size from pine 1 × 10.

❿ Crosscut a 24-in. length of pine 1 × 4 to form the cabinet nailer.

⓫ Sand the shelves, nailer and top panel smooth.

ASSEMBLE THE SIDES & SHELVES

⓬ Lay out and assemble the shelves on the cabinet sides: Note in the *Front Elevation* drawing, page 33, that the bottom shelf is located 8 in. up from the bottom ends of the sides, and the top shelf is spaced 12 in. from the bottom shelf. Mark these positions, then attach the top and bottom shelves to one of the cabinet sides. Spread glue on one end of the top shelf and clamp it to one cabinet side so it aligns with the top shelf reference lines. Drive three 2-in. finish nails through the side and into the end of the top shelf to fasten the parts together **(See Photo D).** Repeat this process to attach the bottom shelf to the same side.

⓭ Install the other cabinet side: Spread glue on the other ends of the two shelves and clamp the remaining cabinet side in place, so the shelves align with their respective shelf reference marks **(See Photo E).**

INSTALL THE NAILER, APRON & BOTTOM TRIM

⓮ Fasten the nailer between the cabinet sides with glue and 2-in. nails. Position the nailer so it is flush with the top ends and back edges of the cabinet sides (See the *Side Section View* drawing, page 33).

⓯ Glue and nail the bottom trim piece in place between the cabinet sides. Position the bottom trim so the scallop profiles face the top of the project and the workpiece is flush with the back edges and bottom ends of the sides.

⓰ Install the apron: Spread glue on the ends of the apron, slip it in place between the cabinet sides flush with the top ends and front edges of the sides. Fasten the parts with nails driven through the cabinet sides **(See Photo F).**

⓱ Recess the nailheads that secure the shelves, nailer, bottom trim and apron with a nailset.

PHOTO E: Spread glue on the free ends of the shelves, clamp the second cabinet side in place and fasten the parts with more 2-in. finish nails.

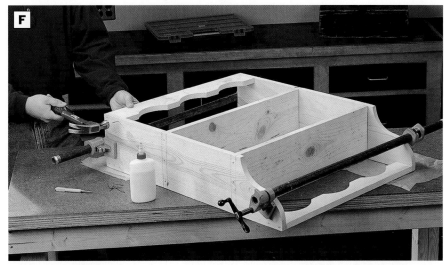

PHOTO F: Install the nailer, apron and bottom trim piece with glue and 2-in. finish nails. Recess all the nailheads with a nailset.

PHOTO G: Using wire brads, attach the beadboard back panel to the back edges of the cabinet sides and shelves as well as to the nailer and bottom trim piece. Set the heads of the brads.

PHOTO H: Position the top on the cabinet so it is flush with the cabinet back and overhangs evenly on the sides and front. Glue, clamp and nail the top in place. Set the nailheads.

PHOTO I: Cut the front and side molding pieces to length. Form 45° mitered corners where the molding wraps around the front of the cabinet by cutting the ends of the molding in a miter box.

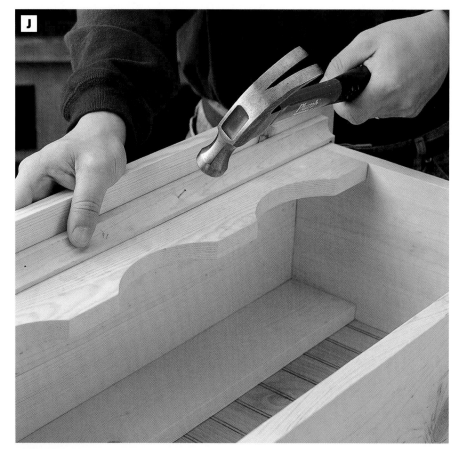

PHOTO J: Fasten the front and side molding pieces to the cabinet with glue and 1½-in. finish nails. Drive the nails at an angle up and into the cabinet top.

INSTALL THE BACK, TOP & COVE MOLDING

18 Lay out and cut the beadboard back panel to size with a circular saw or jig saw. Try to position the long cuts for sizing the panel to width so they split the beaded pattern evenly. Otherwise, the panel will look out of balance once it's installed in the project.

19 Fasten the back panel to the back edges of the shelves and sides as well as to the nailer and bottom trim with ¾-in. brads. Set the brad heads **(See Photo G).**

20 Install the top: Set the top panel in place on the cabinet so it is flush with the back face of the back panel and overhangs the cabinet sides and front evenly. Mark the cabinet position on the top. Spread glue on the mating parts, and clamp the top in place. Secure the top to the cabinet with 2-in. finish nails **(See Photo H).**

㉑ Install the cove molding: Cross-cut the front and two side molding pieces to length. Mark the ends of the front molding piece with 45° miters. Mark the front ends of the side molding pieces with 45° miters as well. Cut the miters using a miter box or a hand saw **(See Photo I).**

㉒ Dry-fit the molding strips in place around the cabinet and beneath the top. Adjust the fit of the mitered ends by lightly filing or sanding them a little at a time until the joints close.

㉓ Fasten the cove molding to the cabinet with glue and 1½-in. finish nails **(See Photo J).**

INSTALL THE TOWEL ROD
㉔ Cut the towel rod dowel to length. Mark the towel rod locations on the outer faces of the cabinet sides (See the *Side Section* drawing, page 33).

㉕ Position the dowel between the sides so it is centered on its reference marks. Drill a pilot hole at your towel rod reference marks and into the ends of the rod. Pin the towel rod in place with a 2-in. finish nail driven into each pilot hole **(See Photo K).**

FINISHING TOUCHES
㉖ Fill nailhead recesses with wood putty and sand smooth.

㉗ If you plan to stain your wall cabinet, brush on a coat of wood conditioner first. Wood conditioner will help the stain penetrate more evenly on softwoods like pine **(See Photo L).**

㉘ Apply your choice of stain, followed by two or three coats of varnish **(See Photo M).**

PHOTO K: Cut the towel rod to fit between the cabinet sides and mark its position. Install the rod with a 2-in. finish nail driven through the cabinet sides and into each end of the dowel. Drill pilot holes for the nails first to keep from splitting the dowel.

PHOTO L (Optional): If you plan to stain the project, it's a good idea to brush on a coat of wood conditioner first. Stain tends to penetrate softwoods like pine unevenly, resulting in a blotchy appearance. Wood conditioner will make the stain penetrate more evenly.

PHOTO M: Brush or wipe on a coat of stain while the wood conditioner is still wet. Allow the stain a few minutes to penetrate into the wood, then wipe off the excess with a clean rag. When the stain dries, apply a clear topcoat.

Kid-size Picnic Table

Children are sure to enjoy this piece of picnic furniture built especially for them. Made of cedar, the project is sized so four children can sit comfortably. Whether you put the table outdoors or bring it inside, it may well become the kids' favorite spot for lunch and dinner. And with no sharp corners or free-standing, tippy benches to cause injuries, you can rest easily, too.

Kid-size Picnic Table: Step-by-step

LAY OUT & CUT THE FRAME PARTS

❶ Crosscut the legs, top and seat stringers and stretcher to length. Cedar is easy to cut with a jig saw, but you'll get straighter cuts using a circular saw.

❷ Lay out the legs: Refer to the *Leg Layout* drawing, page 40, to mark one end of each leg for cutting the top angle. To mark the legs for curved feet, set your compass to a 1¾-in. radius, and determine the centerpoint of the arc on all four legs. Draw the curved feet.

PHOTO A: Lay out the legs and stringers. Scribe the curved end of the legs and the curves on the stringers with a compass, set to the radii given in the technical drawings on page 40.

Kid-size Picnic Table

2" deck screws

2³/₄" rad.

A

B

D

C

A

E

A

D

C

D

B

D

2¹/₂" deck screws

3" deck screws

2¹/₂" deck screws

Leg Layout

2⁵/₁₆"

18"

15⁵/₈"

Top of seat stringer

30⁷/₈"

D

3¹/₂"

LEG LAYOUT

1³/₄" rad., typ.

2³/₄" rad., typ

A

5¹/₂"

1/8"

B

1"

D

D

A

8"

C

26"

13"

1"

SIDE ELEVATION

Kid-size Picnic Table Cutting List			
Part	**No.**	**Size**	**Material**
A. Top slats/seats	7	³/₄ × 5¹/₂ × 48 in.	Cedar
B. Top stringers	2	1¹/₂ × 3¹/₂ × 26 in.	"
C. Seat stringers	2	1¹/₂ × 3¹/₂ × 42 in.	"
D. Legs	4	1¹/₂ × 3¹/₂ × 31 in.	"
E. Stretcher	1	1¹/₂ × 3¹/₂ × 36 in.	"

❸ Lay out the top stringers and seat stringers. Like the legs, these pieces also receive rounded ends. However, only the bottom corners of the stringers are curved—the top corners remain flat to support either the seats or the top slats. Reset your compass to draw a 2¾-in. radius, and scribe the curves on the stringers **(See Photo A).**

❹ Cut the legs and stringers to shape with a jig saw. Guide the saw against a clamped straight-edge to cut the leg angles.

ASSEMBLE THE FRAME

❺ Connect the top stringers and legs. First, find the center along the length of each top stringer, and mark this point on the top flat edge. Then arrange the legs in pairs on your worksurface with the top angled ends forming a straight line and the legs splaying apart in a "V" configuration. Set a top stringer in place on each pair of legs so the top edges of the stringers are flush with the top ends of the legs. Tack the stringer to each leg with a single counter-sunk 2½-in. deck screw. (You'll drive additional screws into these joints once the seat stringers are positioned and fastened.)

❻ Install the seat stringers on the leg assemblies: Mark the seat stringer locations on the legs, according to the *Leg Layout* drawing, page 40. Set the seat stringers on the leg assemblies so the top edges of the stringers align with the leg reference lines. Pivot the legs in or out slightly so the distance from the outside edges of the legs to each end of the seat stringers is 8 in. Secure the top and seat stringers with counter-sunk 2½-in. deck screws, four screws per joint **(See Photo B).**

PHOTO B: Set pairs of legs on your worksurface so they splay outward with their angled ends aligned. Attach the top stringers flush to the tops of the legs, and install the seat stringers so they overhang the legs by 8 in. on each end. Fasten the parts with countersunk 2½-in. deck screws to form two leg assemblies.

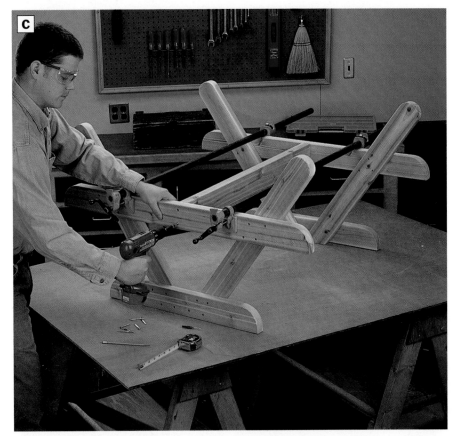

PHOTO C: Stand the leg assemblies top-down to attach the stretcher between them. Hold the stretcher in place with clamps so it is centered on the length of the seat stringers. Drive coun-tersunk 3-in. screws through the seat stringers and into the ends of the stretcher.

PHOTO D: Set the frame upright on the floor to secure the seats into position. The ends of the seats should overhang the seat stringers by about 4½ in. Make the outside edges of the seats overhang the ends of the seat stringers by 1 in.

PHOTO E: After setting the slats into position on the top stretchers and marking alignment lines for screw holes, insert spacers between the slats—we used ¼-in.-thick hardboard. Clamp the top slats together to keep them aligned, and fasten them to the top stringers with countersunk 2-in. deck screws.

7 Complete the frame by joining the leg assemblies to the stretcher: Stand the leg assemblies upside down on your worksurface, and clamp the stretcher to the seat stringers so it's centered on their lengths. Drive pairs of 3-in. countersunk deck screws through the seat stringers and into the ends of the stretcher to fasten the parts **(See Photo C).**

PREPARE & ATTACH THE SEATS

8 Crosscut the seats to length.

9 Scribe the rounded ends on the seats with a compass set to draw a 2¾-in. radius.

10 Cut the rounds ends of the seat boards with a jig saw. Smooth the curves with a file.

11 Attach the seats to the frame: The ends of the seats should extend past the seat stringers equal amounts on both sides (about 4½ in.). Let the outside edges of the seat boards overhang the ends of the seat stringers by 1 in. With the seats in position, fasten the parts with countersunk 2½-in. deck screws driven through the seats and into the seat stringers **(See Photo D).**

INSTALL THE TOP SLATS

12 Cut the five top slats to length and set them in place on the two top stringers so they overhang the stringers evenly. Don't worry about spacing between the slats yet. With a straightedge, draw lines for screw holes across the slats to mark the centerlines of the top stringers.

13 Fasten the slats to the top stringers: Insert scrap spacers between the slats first to provide for even spacing (we used ¼-in. hardboard for spacers). Because not all dimensional lumber is precisely the same width, you may need to determine the spacing between your slats according to the boards you're using. Clamp the top slats together to hold them in place. Drill pairs of countersunk pilot holes through the slats along the stringer marks, and install the slats with 2-in. deck screws **(See Photo E)**.

14 Set your compass for a 2¾-in. radius, and scribe curves onto the outer four corners of the table top. Cut the corner curves, and file the cut edges smooth **(See Photo F)**.

FINISHING TOUCHES

15 Sand all exposed project surfaces with a random-orbit sander and 150-grit sandpaper **(See Photo G)**.

EDITOR'S NOTE: *We left this project bare rather than finishing with an exterior topcoat, because most of these products aren't safe for use on eating surfaces.*

PHOTO F: Mark a 2¾-in. radius on each of the four corners of the tabletop, and trim the corners with a jig saw.

PHOTO G: Since cedar is prone to splintering, you'll want to give the table a good sanding to break the edges and smooth the parts. A random-orbit sander is the best tool for the job. It's a good idea to wear a dust mask when sanding cedar; the dust can be a respiratory irritant.

Tool Tote

Keep your workshop, craft or gardening supplies and tools close at hand with this portable tool tote. We've kept the design simple and straightforward, just the way plumbers and carpenters have built them for generations. If your handyman pursuits find you wiring one day but framing a shed or plumbing a sink the next, make a tote for every task. Your tools will be collected and organized when duty calls.

Shopping List

- ☐ (1) 1 × 8 in. × 10 ft. pine
- ☐ (1) 1-in.-dia. × 36-in. dowel
- ☐ (1) ¼-in.-dia. × 6-in. dowel
- ☐ 2-in. drywall screws
- ☐ Wood glue
- ☐ Finishing materials

Tool Tote: Step-by-step

MAKE THE PARTS

❶ Crosscut two 24-in. lengths of pine for the front and back tote panels, as well as a 22½-in. workpiece for the tote bottom.

❷ Crosscut two 14-in.-long pine boards for the tote ends. Lay out the angled portions on each end with a straightedge, according to the *End Layout* drawing, page 46.

❸ Cut the two end pieces to shape with a jig saw or circular saw. Clamp each workpiece to your worksurface to hold it securely while you cut.

❹ Drill the dowel-handle holes: Find the centerpoint for drilling the handle dowel hole through each tote

Backer board

PHOTO A: Clamp a backer board beneath each tote end before drilling the 1-in.-dia. holes for the dowel handle. A backer board will keep the drill bit from tearing out wood as it exits the hole.

Tool Tote

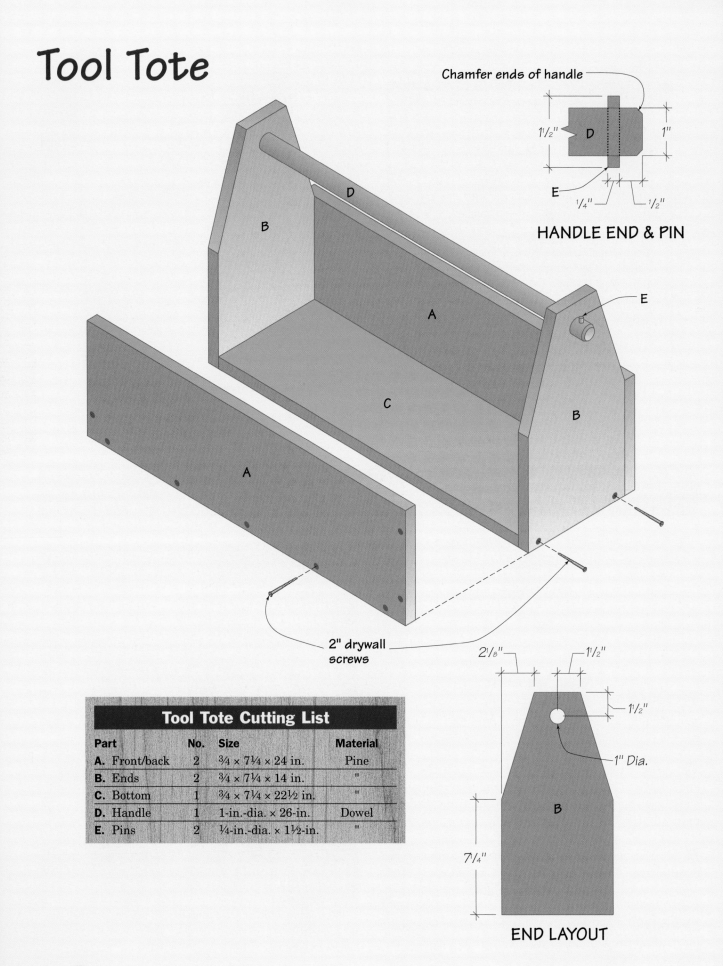

Chamfer ends of handle

1½"   D   1"

E   ¼"   ½"

HANDLE END & PIN

D

B

A

C

A

E

B

2" drywall
screws

2⅛"   1½"

1½"

1" Dia.

B

7¼"

END LAYOUT

Tool Tote Cutting List

Part	No.	Size	Material
A. Front/back	2	¾ × 7¼ × 24 in.	Pine
B. Ends	2	¾ × 7¼ × 14 in.	"
C. Bottom	1	¾ × 7¼ × 22½ in.	"
D. Handle	1	1-in.-dia. × 26-in.	Dowel
E. Pins	2	¼-in.-dia. × 1½-in.	"

PHOTO B: Drill ¼-in.-dia. holes through the handle dowel, ½ in. in from each end. A shop-made cradle jig with V-notches will help you steady the dowel while you drill.

PHOTO C: Fasten the tote ends, bottom, front and back together with glue and 2-in. drywall screws. Slip the dowel handle into place and secure it with two handle pins, glued and tapped into place.

end. The dowel should be centered side-to-side on the end pieces, 1½ in. down from the top. Clamp a scrap backer board beneath each end before drilling the holes to keep the drill bit from tearing out the wood as it exits. Drill the holes with a 1-in.-dia. spade bit **(See Photo A)**. Sand the holes to enlarge them slightly so the dowel handle will swivel.

MAKE THE HANDLE

❺ Mark and crosscut the dowel handle to length with a jig saw. Clamp the dowel securely while you cut. Sand the dowel ends to form chamfers.

❻ Drill a ¼-in.-dia. hole through the handle dowel, ½ in. from each end for the handle pins. You'll find that it's difficult to drill these holes straight unless you can keep the dowel from rolling while you drill. We built a simple cradle jig with V-notches on both ends to hold the dowel steady **(See Photo B)**. Make the jig about 10 to 12 in. long. With the dowel handle in the jig, bore a hole for each handle pin.

ASSEMBLE THE TOTE

❼ Glue and fasten the tote ends to the ends of the bottom panel with countersunk 2-in. drywall screws.

❽ Glue and screw the tote front and back to the ends and bottom.

❾ Attach the handle: Slip the dowel handle through the holes in the tote ends. Cut two 1½-in. dowel pins and sand the ends smooth. Spread glue on the pins

and tap them through the holes in the handle with a hammer or mallet until the pins protrude evenly from the handle **(See Photo C)**.

Adding tote organizers

This tote project can be left as is, with the center compartment open for holding longer tools and supplies. However, smaller items and tools will be easier to find if you install additional partitions inside the tote. We used scrap wood left over from the project to make individual compartments for separating wrenches, chisels, snips and a drill/driver. A strip of wood with a series of ¼-in. holes drilled through it provides a handy way to store screwdrivers. Organize your tote as you see fit for the tools you use the most.

Spice Shelves

Get those jars of spices and seasoning out of a dark cupboard and onto this handsome oak spice holder. Two lower shelves are designed to accommodate full-size shakers, while the top shelf stores taller containers and bottles. Chamfered back slats and lap-jointed front rails lend a fine woodworking air to this deceptively simple piece.

Spice Shelves: Step-by-step

MAKE THE BACK PANEL

❶ Crosscut the four back slats to length: Arrange the slats together on edge to form a panel with pleasing grain pattern. Label the order of the slats in the panel.

❷ Mill the back slat chamfers with a router and a piloted chamfering bit: Set the bit to a depth of ⅛ in. Rout only the "show-side" edges of the slats that will touch each other once the back panel is glued up. The two outermost edges are not chamfered (**See Photo A**).

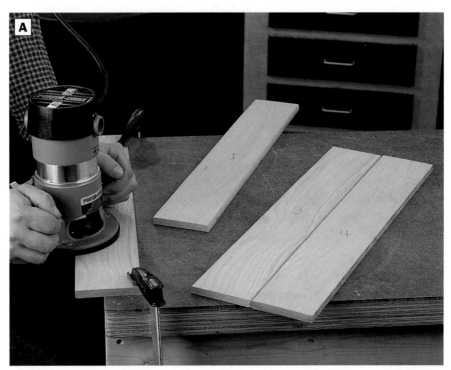

PHOTO A: Rout chamfers along the mating edges of the back slats with a piloted chamfering bit set to a cutting depth of ⅛ in. It's a good idea to label the slats first so you profile only the edges that will meet once the panel is glued up.

Spice Shelves

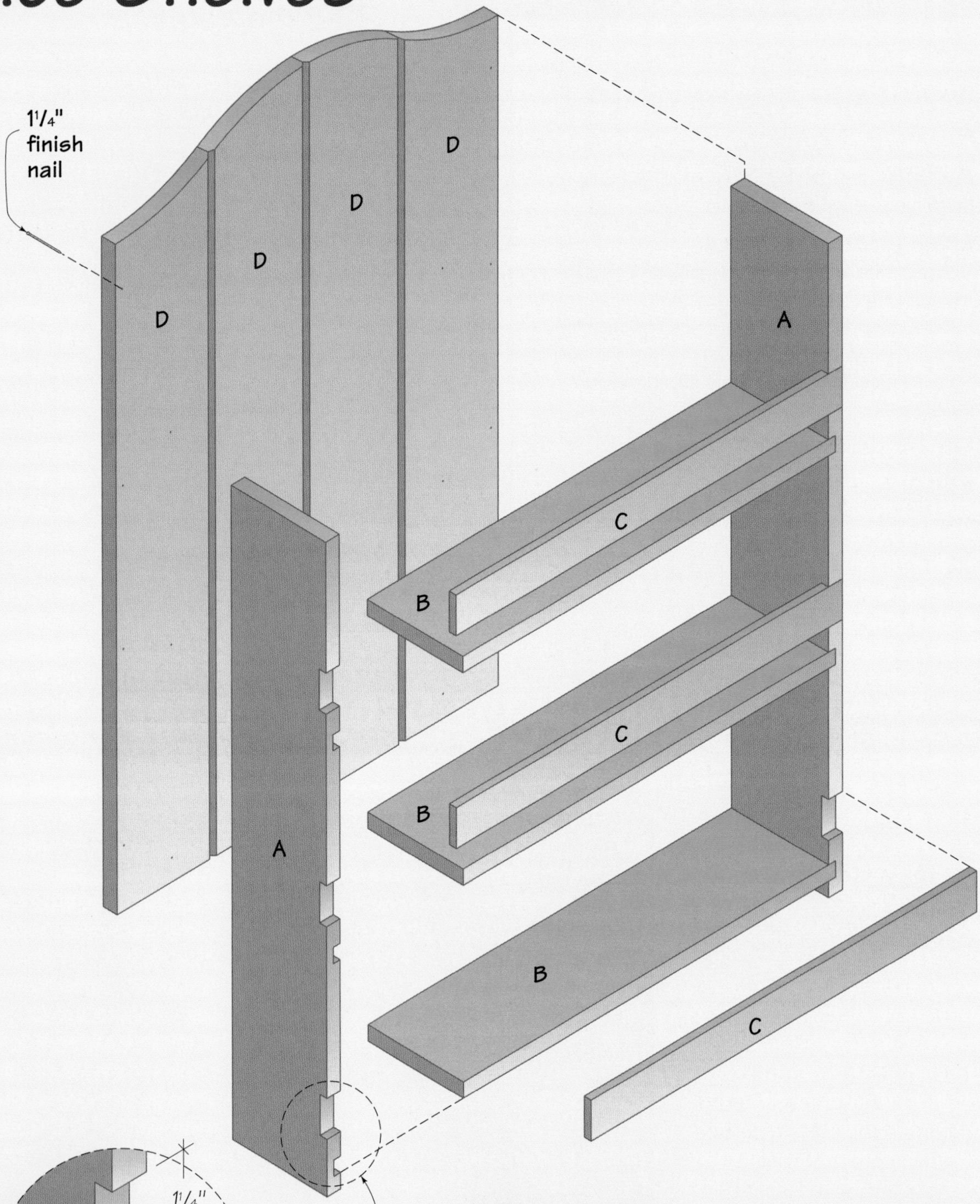

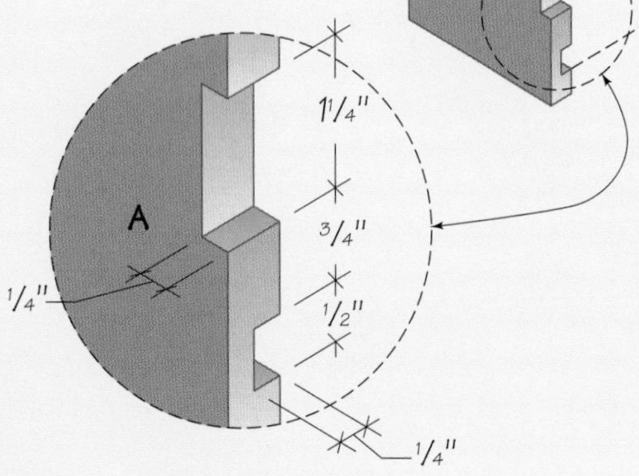

1¼" finish nail

D

D

D

D

D

A

C

B

C

B

A

B

C

SIDE - NOTCH & DADO DETAIL

A

1¼"

3/4"

1/2"

1/4"

1/4"

Spice Shelves Cutting List			
Part	**No.**	**Size**	**Material**
A. Sides	2	½ × 3½ × 20 in.	Red oak
B. Shelves	3	½ × 3½ × 13⅝ in.	"
C. Front rails	3	¼ × 1¼ × 14³⁄₁₆ in.	"
D. Back slats	4	½ × 3½ × 22 in.	"

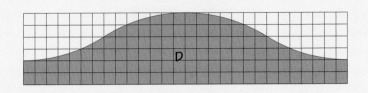

½" squares

BACK CURVE LAYOUT

BACK V-GROOVE

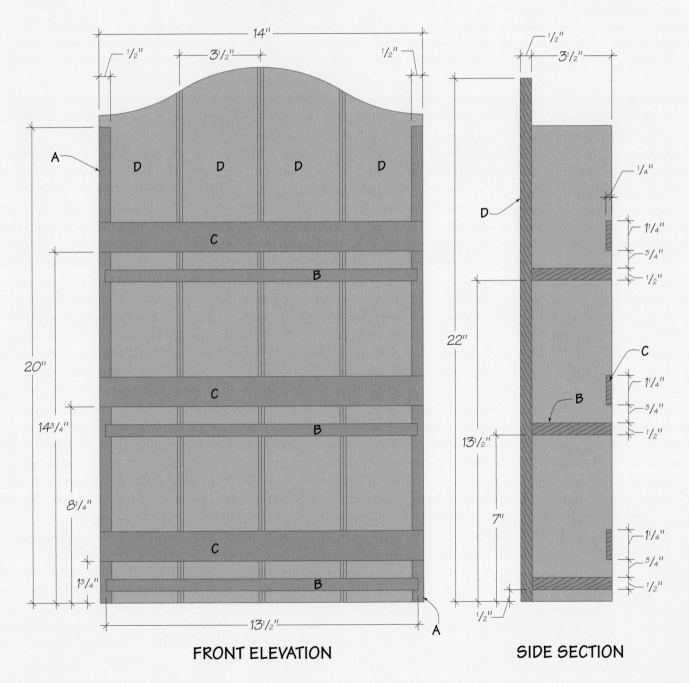

FRONT ELEVATION

SIDE SECTION

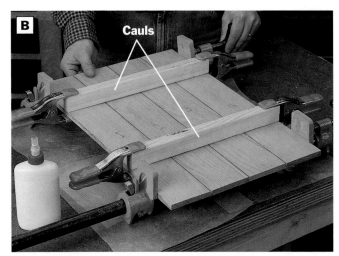

PHOTO B: Glue and clamp the slats together to form the back panel. Clamp scrap cauls across the slats to hold the panels flat. Apply just enough clamping pressure to close the joints.

PHOTO C: Enlarge the *Back Curve Layout* grid pattern on page 51 to make a template for drawing the profile at the top of the back. Cut the profile to shape with a jig saw.

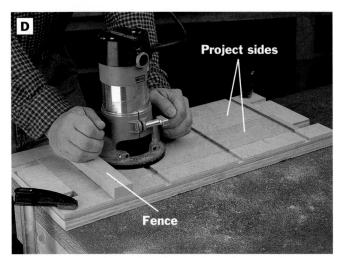

PHOTO D: Create a simple shop-made jig out of plywood to gang-rout shelf dadoes across the sides. Guide the router base along a removable fence, and rout each dado clear across both the jig and sides.

PHOTO E: Spread glue on the mating surfaces of the shelves and sides, and assemble these parts. NOTE: *In this photo, the rail notches in the sides are facing down.*

3 Glue up the back panel: Spread wood glue along the mating edges of the chamfered back slats and clamp them together. Also clamp a pair of scrap cauls across the panel to help keep it flat (**See Photo B**).

4 Create a full-size paper template of the *Back Curve Layout,* page 51, and use the template to trace the top profile onto the back panel. Trim the top profile to shape with a jig saw (**See Photo C**).

5 Sand the back panel smooth with 150-grit paper. It's easier to sand this panel now before assembly.

MAKE THE SIDES

6 Crosscut the sides to length. Lay out the shelf dadoes on these workpieces, positioning them according to the *Side Section* drawing, page 51.

7 Rout shelf dadoes in the sides. We routed the dado grooves across both sides at once with a simple shop-made jig. The jig is comprised of a ¾-in. plywood panel about 12 in. wide and 24 in. long, sized so that both side panels can lie side by side and flat on it. Strips of ½-in.-thick plywood were glued (not nailed) around the panel to hold both side panels securely and to serve as back-up support for minimizing bit tearout. We then screwed a fence across the jig to guide the router base for cutting the dadoes. With the jig clamped to your worksurface and the sides in place, rout dado grooves across the full jig and both sides at your shelf layout marks, moving the jig fence accordingly for making each dado cut (**See Photo D**).

8 Lay out and cut the ¼-in.-deep, 1¼-in.-wide notches in the sides that will house the three front

PHOTO F: Dry-fit the front rails in their notches in the sides. The rails should fit flush with the front edges of the sides. Once they do, glue and clamp the front rails in the notches.

PHOTO G: The back is secured with glue and nails. Before attaching, mark a line across the back at each shelf to serve as guides for locating the fasteners. Drill pilot holes for the finish nails, and set the heads so they will not scratch the wall once the shelf unit is hung.

rails. See the *Front Elevation* drawing, page 51, for marking the notch locations, then carefully cut the notches with a sharp wood chisel.

⑨ Smooth the sides with 150-grit sandpaper.

ASSEMBLE THE PROJECT

⑩ Dry-fit the shelves in the side dadoes to check the fit of the parts. Widen or deepen the dadoes as needed with a chisel and sandpaper.

⑪ Apply glue to the ends of the shelves and into the dadoes, then assemble the shelves and sides with clamps. Tighten the clamps just enough to seat the shelves in the dadoes (**See Photo E**).

⑫ Cut the front rails to length and dry-fit them in their notches on the sides. Adjust the fit of the parts as needed by chiseling out more waste from the notches. The rails should fit flush with the front edges of the sides.

⑬ Spread glue into the notches and install the rails, clamping the parts together (**See Photo F**).

⑭ Fasten the back panel to the project: Turn the project facedown on your worksurface. Set the back in place with the chamfered face down and mark shelf centerlines across the back for locating finish nails. Spread glue on the back edges of the sides and shelves, and set the back panel in place. Install the back with 1¼-in. finish nails driven through pilot holes in the shelves and sides (**See Photo G**).

FINISHING TOUCHES

⑮ Apply the finish of your choice. We wiped on three coats of Danish oil.

⑯ Attach picture hanger hardware that will allow the spice rack to hang close to the wall.

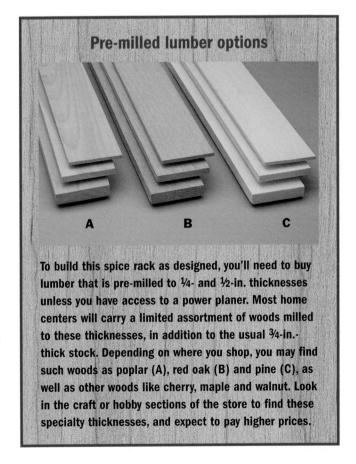

Pre-milled lumber options

A   B   C

To build this spice rack as designed, you'll need to buy lumber that is pre-milled to ¼- and ½-in. thicknesses unless you have access to a power planer. Most home centers will carry a limited assortment of woods milled to these thicknesses, in addition to the usual ¾-in.-thick stock. Depending on where you shop, you may find such woods as poplar (A), red oak (B) and pine (C), as well as other woods like cherry, maple and walnut. Look in the craft or hobby sections of the store to find these specialty thicknesses, and expect to pay higher prices.

2 × 4 Workbench

Agood workbench should be generously proportioned, yet small enough to fit into cramped working quarters. It should be solidly constructed, yet light enough to move around the shop. The best benches make use of the space below the top for shelving and storage. We took all of these considerations seriously when designing this workbench. Its reinforced hardboard top provides a smooth, sizable worksurface that's easy to replace. The laminated 2 × 4 legs will support even your heaviest projects. When you're done working, tuck the bench against a wall and use the bottom shelf for storage.

Vital statistics

TYPE: Workbench

OVERALL SIZE: 24W by 36H by 60L

MATERIAL: Pine, plywood, hardboard

JOINERY: Butt joints reinforced with screws

CONSTRUCTION DETAILS:
· Legs are made of pairs of 2 × 4s face-glued and screwed together
· Hardboard worksurface is attached to plywood sub-top with finish nails only so it can be replaced when the surface wears out

FINISH: Clear protective topcoat or none

BUILDING TIME: 4-6 hours

Shopping List

☐ (1) ¼ in. × 4 × 8 ft. hardboard
☐ (7) 2 × 4 in. × 8 ft. pine
☐ (1) ¾ in. × 4 × 8 ft. plywood
☐ Deck screws (1¼-, 2-, 2½-, 3-in.)
☐ 1½-in. finish nails
☐ Wood glue
☐ Finishing materials (optional)

2 × 4 Workbench: Step-by-step

CUT THE PARTS

❶ Cut the legs, stretchers, rails and crossbrace to length.

❷ Cut the sub-top, shelf and work-surface parts to size.

MAKE THE LEG ASSEMBLIES

❸ Build the legs by gluing and screwing pairs of leg pieces together. Be sure the edges and ends of the parts are flush, and stagger the screw pattern.

❹ Join the legs and rails: Turn the legs over so the screwheads face

PHOTO A: Attach the top and shelf rails to the legs with 3-in. deck screws to create two leg assemblies. The top rails should be flush with the tops of the legs. Fasten the shelf rails so their top edges are 11¾ in. up from the leg bottoms.

down on your worksurface. Position a top rail so it's flush with the top ends of a pair of legs. Set the shelf rails so the top edges are 11¾ in. up from the leg bottoms. Attach the rails to the legs with 3-in. deck screws to form the leg assemblies (**See Photo A**).

2 × 4 Workbench

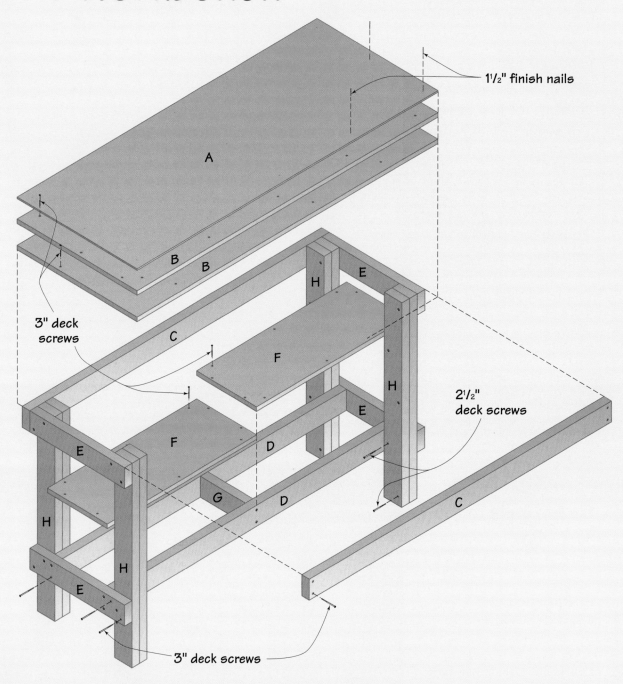

1½" finish nails

3" deck screws

2½" deck screws

3" deck screws

A

B

B

C

D

D

E

E

E

E

F

F

G

H

H

H

H

2 × 4 Workbench Cutting List								
Part	**No.**	**Size**	**Material**		**Part**	**No.**	**Size**	**Material**
A. Worksurface	1	¼ × 24 × 60 in.	Hardboard		**E.** Top/shelf rails	4	1½ × 3½ × 19 in.	Pine
B. Sub-top	2	¾ × 24 × 60 in.	Plywood		**F.** Shelf sections	2	¾ × 12 × 30 in.	Plywood
C. Top stretchers	2	1½ × 3½ × 60 in.	Pine		**G.** Crossbrace	1	1½ × 3½ × 9 in.	Pine
D. Shelf stretchers	2	1½ × 3½ × 57 in.	"		**H.** Legs	8	1½ × 3½ × 34½ in.	"

PHOTO B: Build the shelf assembly by attaching the shelf stretchers to the crossbrace first, then clamp the shelf frame between the legs, even with the shelf rails. Drive 3-in. deck screws through the shelf rails into the ends of the shelf stretchers.

PHOTO C: Center the sub-top over the top stretchers, allowing for an even overhang, front to back. The ends of the sub-top are flush with the top rails. Secure the sub-top to the top stretchers and rails with 3-in. deck screws.

ASSEMBLE THE BENCH & SHELF FRAMES

Because of the size of the workbench, continue the assembly working on the floor.

5 Set the leg assemblies on edge to attach the top stretchers. These stretchers should sit flush with the tops of the leg assemblies and overlap the ends of the top rails. Install the top stretchers with countersunk 3-in. deck screws driven into the ends of the top rails.

6 Assemble the shelf stretchers and crossbrace according to the technical drawing on page 56. Position the crossbrace so it is centered on the shelf stretchers, and attach the parts with 3-in. deck screws.

7 With the bench assembly on its side, install the shelf frame between the legs and shelf rails. Align the ends of the shelf stretchers with the shelf rails, and clamp the parts together. Fasten the shelf frame to the bench with 3-in. deck screws driven through the side rails **(See Photo B).**

ATTACH THE SHELF & TOP

8 Screw the two shelf sections to the shelf stretchers, shelf rails and crossbrace. Use countersunk 2-in. deck screws.

9 Laminate the two plywood sub-top pieces together with glue and 1¼-in. screws.

10 Install the sub-top: Center the sub-top on the top stretchers and align the ends of the sub-top with the

outside faces of the top rails. Attach the parts by driving 3-in. countersunk deck screws through the sub-top into the stretchers and rails **(See Photo C).**

11 Attach the worksurface, aligning it evenly with the sub-top all around. Use 1½-in. finish nails, spaced evenly around the perimeter, to secure the hardboard to the sub-top **(See Photo D).** Recess the nailheads with a nailset.

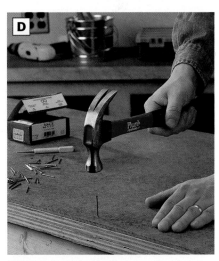

PHOTO D: Tack the hardboard worksurface to the sub-top with 1½-in. finish nails. Set the nailheads to create a flat bench surface.

FINISHING TOUCHES

12 Round over the corners of the worksurface and sub-top: Cut off the sharp corners with a jig saw or circular saw, then smooth the profiles with a coarse file and sandpaper until they're round and even.

13 Apply several coats of wood finish, if you wish, to help protect the bench from stains and abrasions. We brushed on two coats of Danish oil, but varnish also would be a good choice.

Sawhorses

Sawhorses may well be a handyman's most trusted companion. They create a durable worksurface wherever you need it, whether in the shop or in the field. This sturdy, shop-tested model, made of 2 × 4s and plywood, features a shelf beneath to keep necessary tools and supplies handy. Although one of these horses can be a great help, build a pair to create your own "work crew"—without paying them hourly wages!

Vital statistics

TYPE: Sawhorses

OVERALL SIZE: 24W by 30H by 38L

MATERIAL: Pine, plywood

JOINERY: Butt joints reinforced with screws

CONSTRUCTION DETAILS:
· Legs are miter-cut near their top ends to form the A-shaped leg spread
· Plywood gussets reinforce the leg joints

FINISH: None or a clear protective topcoat

BUILDING TIME: 6-8 hours (for two)

Shopping List (for two)

☐ (2) ¾ × ¾ in. × 8 ft. quarter-round molding

☐ (4) 2 × 4 in. × 8 ft. pine

☐ (1) 2 × 6 in. × 8 ft. pine

☐ (2) ¾ in. × 2 × 4 ft. plywood

☐ Deck screws (2-, 2½-, 3-in.)

☐ 1¼-in. galvanized finish nails

Sawhorses: Step-by-step

PHOTO A: Assemble pairs of legs with a plywood gusset, keeping the gusset flush with the top and outside edges of the legs. Flip the assembly over and install the shelf support so the ends are flush with the outside edges of the legs (about 10 in. up from the leg bottoms).

CUT THE PARTS TO SIZE

① Crosscut the top plate, legs and shelf supports to length. Cut the plywood gussets and shelves to rough size. Miter-cut quarter-round shelf-lip pieces to length.

② Using the three layout drawings on page 60, draw the angles on the legs, shelf supports and gussets. Make these angle cuts with a jig saw or circular saw.

MAKE THE LEG ASSEMBLIES

③ Arrange two legs and a gusset on your worksurface so the top miter cuts of the legs butt together and the angled edges of the gusset are flush with the outside edges of the legs. Join the gussets to the legs with 2-in. deck screws driven through countersunk pilot holes.

Sawhorses

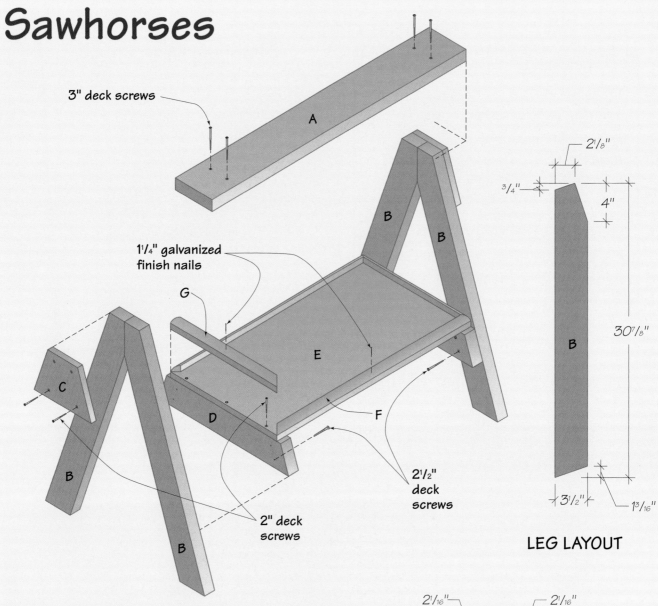

3" deck screws

1¹/₄" galvanized
finish nails

A

B

B

G

C

E

B

D

F

B

2¹/₂"
deck
screws

2" deck
screws

LEG LAYOUT

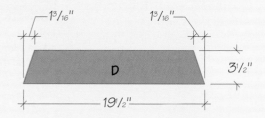

2¹/₈"

³/₄"

4"

B

30⁷/₈"

3¹/₂"

1³/₁₆"

GUSSET LAYOUT

2¹/₁₆"

2¹/₁₆"

C

6"

8⁵/₈"

SHELF SUPPORT LAYOUT

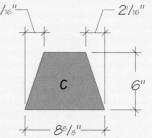

1³/₁₆"

1³/₁₆"

D

3¹/₂"

19¹/₂"

Sawhorses Cutting List (makes two)			
Part	**No.**	**Size**	**Material**
A. Top plates	2	1½ × 5½ × 38 in.	Pine
B. Legs	8	1½ × 3½ × 31 in.	"
C. Gussets	4	¾ × 8⅝ × 6 in.	Plywood
D. Shelf supports	4	1½ × 3½ × 19½ in.	Pine
E. Shelves	2	¾ × 29 × 16 in.	Plywood
F. Shelf lips (long)	4	¾ × ¾ × 29 in.	Quarter-round molding
G. Shelf lips (short)	4	¾ × ¾ × 16 in.	"

4 Flip the leg assembly over to attach the shelf support. Align the angled ends of the shelf support so they're flush with the outside edges of the legs (this should place the shelf support about 10 in. up from the leg bottoms). Fasten the shelf supports to the legs with countersunk 2½-in. deck screws **(See Photo A)**.

5 Repeat Steps 2 through 4 to build the other three leg assemblies.

ATTACH THE SHELF & TOP PLATE
6 Attach the shelf: Stand two leg assemblies upright on the floor so the shelf supports face inward. Set a shelf panel in place on the shelf supports. Hold the parts together with clamps. Fasten the shelf to the shelf supports with countersunk 2-in. deck screws. Do the same for the other sawhorse.

7 Install the top plate. Center the top plate over the leg assemblies. Drill countersunk pilot holes, and drive 3-in. deck screws down through the top plate into the top ends of the legs **(See Photo B)**.

FINISHING TOUCHES
8 Attach the shelf-lip pieces to the shelves to form a shallow tray. Start by nailing a short lip piece in place, and work your way around, matching up the mitered joints as you go. Avoid splitting the narrow quarter-round by drilling pilot holes for the finish nails. Use a nailset to set protruding nailheads **(See Photo C)**.

EDITOR'S NOTE: *If you choose to topcoat these sawhorses, avoid using paint or stain; these finishes could mar other workpieces when the sawhorses are in use. Use a clear protective finish instead, like varnish or tung oil.*

PHOTO B: With the sawhorses standing upright, center each top plate over the legs so it overhangs evenly all around. Drill countersunk pilot holes and secure the top plates to the top ends of the legs with 3-in. deck screws.

PHOTO C: Attach the quarter-round shelf lips to the shelves with 1¼-in. finish nails. Start at a short side, driving the finish nails through pilot holes. Set the nailheads below the surface of the wood with a nailset.

Booster Bench

There's no denying that youngsters love to do things themselves.
Bring sink faucets and higher bookshelves down to their level with
the aid of this booster bench. It also makes a great seat for story time.
Build one with a 4-ft.-long piece of 1×8 in just a couple hours.

Shopping List

☐ (1) 1 × 8 in. × 4 ft. pine

☐ Wood glue

☐ #8 × 2-in. flathead wood screws

Booster Bench: Step-by-step

MAKE THE STRETCHER & LEGS

❶ Rip and crosscut a 2½-in.-wide, 12½-in.-long board for the stretcher. To draw the stretcher arch, use a photocopier to enlarge the curved grid shown on the *Stretcher Layout* drawing, page 64, until the squares are ½ in. Cut out your paper pattern and use it as a template for drawing the stretcher arch on the pine blank.

❷ Crosscut two 6-in. lengths of pine for the legs.

❸ Draw the leg shapes, using the *Leg Layout* grid drawing, page 64, as a guide. Make another paper template and use it to draw the leg arches (**See Photo A**).

PHOTO A: Draw arched profiles on the stretcher and legs. Full-size paper templates are helpful for drawing these curved shapes.

Booster Bench

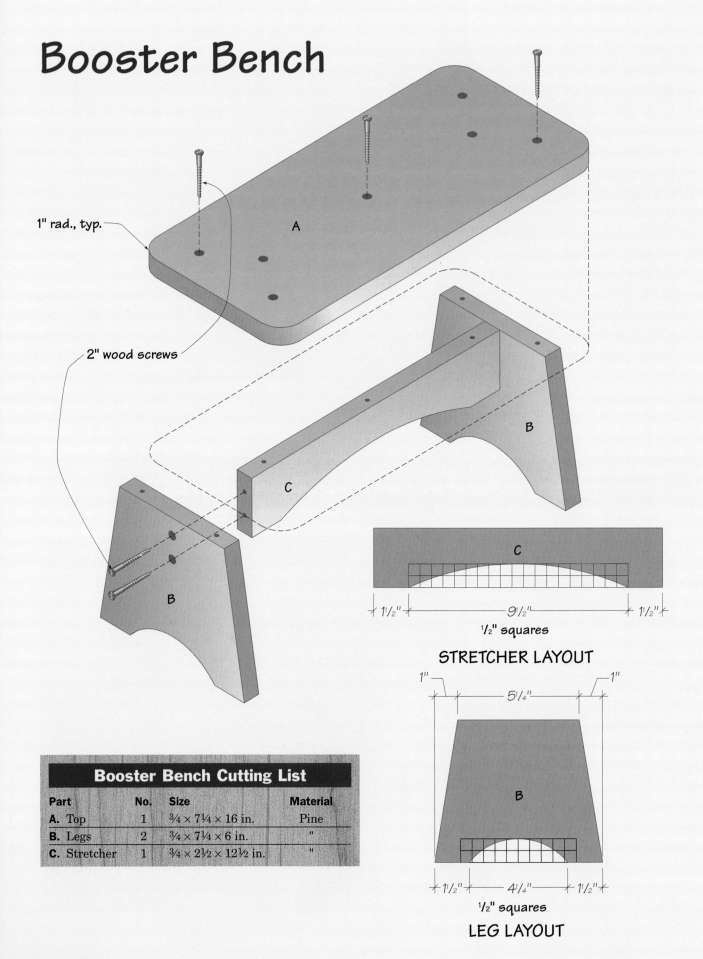

1" rad., typ.

2" wood screws

A

B

C

B

C

1¹⁄₂" 9¹⁄₂" 1¹⁄₂"

¹⁄₂" squares

STRETCHER LAYOUT

1" 5¹⁄₄" 1"

B

1¹⁄₂" 4¹⁄₄" 1¹⁄₂"

¹⁄₂" squares

LEG LAYOUT

Booster Bench Cutting List			
Part	**No.**	**Size**	**Material**
A. Top	1	³⁄₄ × 7¹⁄₄ × 16 in.	Pine
B. Legs	2	³⁄₄ × 7¹⁄₄ × 6 in.	"
C. Stretcher	1	³⁄₄ × 2¹⁄₂ × 12¹⁄₂ in.	"

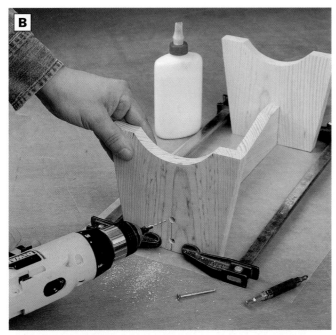

PHOTO B: Glue and clamp the stretcher between the legs so the top ends and edges of the parts are flush. Fasten the parts with countersunk 2-in. flathead wood screws.

④ Cut the arches in the stretchers and legs with a jig saw. Smooth the curved cuts with a file.

MAKE THE TOP

⑤ Crosscut a 16-in. board for the bench top.

⑥ Lay out and draw 1-in. radius corners on the top workpiece. Cut the corners, and smooth the curved cuts with a file.

ASSEMBLE THE BENCH

⑦ Sand all of the stool parts smooth.

⑧ Assemble the stretcher and legs: Draw centerlines on the legs for locating the stretcher and pairs of attachment screws. Spread glue on the ends of the stretcher and clamp it in place between the legs. Drill countersunk pilot holes through the legs and into the stretcher, then fasten the parts with 2-in. flathead wood screws.

⑨ Install the top: Center the top over the legs and stretchers, and mark centerlines on the top for driving screws into the legs and stretcher. Spread glue on the mating parts, and drive countersunk flathead wood screws through the top to join the parts.

⑩ Finish the bench: Fill the screwhead recesses with wood putty, and sand smooth. Apply primer and glossy paint (See *Wood & Finish Options,* right).

PHOTO C: Attach the top to the stretcher and legs with glue and screws. Lay out the stretcher and leg locations on the top first, for locating the screws.

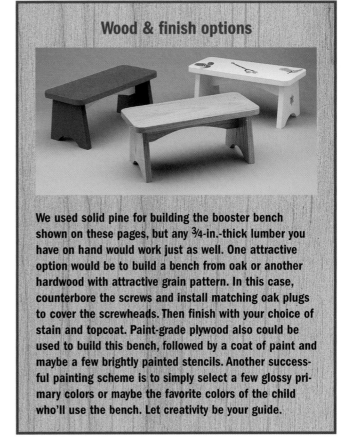

Wood & finish options

We used solid pine for building the booster bench shown on these pages, but any ¾-in.-thick lumber you have on hand would work just as well. One attractive option would be to build a bench from oak or another hardwood with attractive grain pattern. In this case, counterbore the screws and install matching oak plugs to cover the screwheads. Then finish with your choice of stain and topcoat. Paint-grade plywood also could be used to build this bench, followed by a coat of paint and maybe a few brightly painted stencils. Another successful painting scheme is to simply select a few glossy primary colors or maybe the favorite colors of the child who'll use the bench. Let creativity be your guide.

Building Blocks

Play blocks are timeless toys, and they make a great gift. They're also a good solution for using up those odds and ends of hardwood that accumulate in every woodshop. This design includes all the popular shapes of store-bought block sets, and building them is as easy as it looks.

Building Blocks: Step-by-step

LAY OUT & CUT THE BLOCKS

1 Follow the dimensions given in the technical drawings, page 68, to lay out the assorted block shapes. If you build this project with the quantity and size of lumber specified in the *Cutting List,* you'll be able to construct the full set of 56 pieces. We've sized the block shapes so you can lay many of them out side by side or in groups of two or four to maximize lumber. With this in mind, draw all the shapes.

2 Cut out the blocks. A number of the block shapes are small once they're completed, so organize your cutting sequence to allow enough extra lumber to clamp and cut the parts safely.

3 Cut the arch shapes. You could cut these curves with a jig saw, but we used a 3-in. hole saw instead

Child-safe woods & finishes

This play blocks project may seem like the perfect way to clean out your shop scrap bin, but keep a few things in mind: Not all wood types are suitable for making toys for small children. Softwoods like cedar or redwood can splinter if a child chews on them. Treated lumber is manufactured with harmful chemicals that shouldn't be ingested, as are sheet goods like plywood and particleboard. Avoid exotic species as well: some contain natural oils that may irritate skin and eyes. Better wood alternatives for toys are hardwoods like maple, birch and poplar. They resist splintering, contain no potentially harmful chemicals and take finishes well.

Speaking of finishes, most wood finishes are safe for children once they fully dry, but if you plan to paint these blocks, choose paint that's labeled "child-safe" on the can. If a clear finish is what you're after, topcoat the blocks with shellac or water-based polyurethane. You could also simply wipe them with mineral oil, available at all drugstores.

Building Blocks

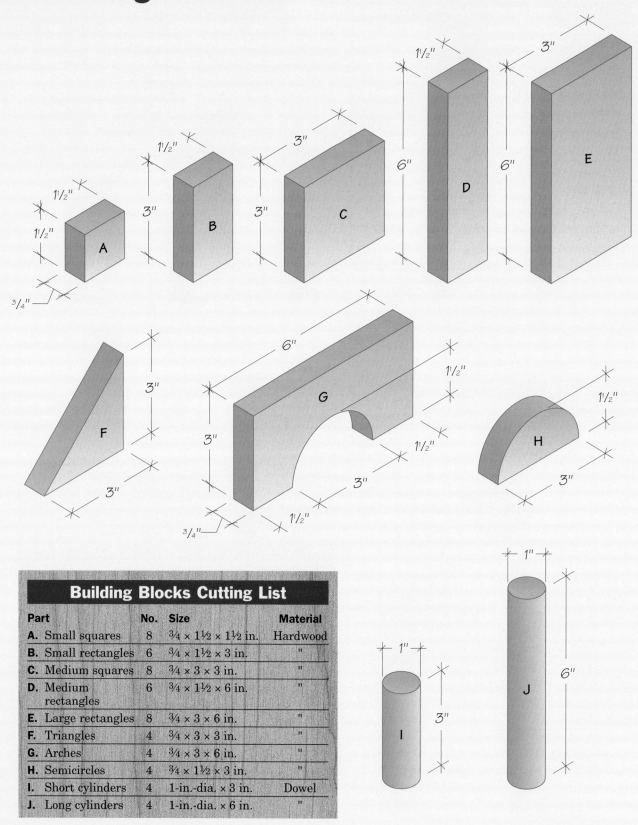

Building Blocks Cutting List

Part	No.	Size	Material
A. Small squares	8	¾ × 1½ × 1½ in.	Hardwood
B. Small rectangles	6	¾ × 1½ × 3 in.	"
C. Medium squares	8	¾ × 3 × 3 in.	"
D. Medium rectangles	6	¾ × 1½ × 6 in.	"
E. Large rectangles	8	¾ × 3 × 6 in.	"
F. Triangles	4	¾ × 3 × 3 in.	"
G. Arches	4	¾ × 3 × 6 in.	"
H. Semicircles	4	¾ × 1½ × 3 in.	"
I. Short cylinders	4	1-in.-dia. × 3 in.	Dowel
J. Long cylinders	4	1-in.-dia. × 6 in.	"

PHOTO A: Lay out and cut the block shapes. Arrange the parts on your boards to maximize the lumber. We cut the curved profiles of the arch blocks with a 3-in. hole saw.

PHOTO B: Sand the blocks thoroughly to remove all sharp corners, edges and any splinters.

to produce smooth arch shapes **(See Photo A).**

❹ Mark and cut the dowel rod for making the long and short cylinders. Clamp the dowel securely if you cut the cylinders with a jig saw. You may find it easier to cut these parts with a fine-toothed hand saw instead.

FINISHING TOUCHES

❺ Sand the blocks thoroughly with 150-grit sandpaper. Remove all sharp corners and edges **(See Photo B).**

❻ Apply the finish. We sprayed on a coat of primer first, followed by two coats of child-safe enamel paint in assorted primary colors **(See Photo C).** Sand lightly between coats of paint to smooth the surfaces further.

PHOTO C: Finish the blocks. We used primer and child-safe enamel spray paint. To make spraying easier, we hung the blocks with thumbtacks and string attached to a scrap of wood and suspended over a cardboard spraying shield. Wear a respirator if you use a spray finish.

Entry Bench

This Shaker-inspired slat-back bench offers perfect occasional seating in any room. Made from a single sheet of plywood, the project comfortably seats three adults, yet it is light enough for one person to carry or move with ease.

Entry Bench: Step-by-step

The unique feature of this bench is that the stretcher and legs are notched where they join together to form half-lap joints. Half-lap joints help keep the legs from racking once the bench is assembled and allow the stretcher to pass through the legs in essentially one piece.

MAKE THE LEGS & SEAT

1 Cut the legs to rough size. In order to build the bench from one sheet of plywood, it is necessary to lay out two legs along the length of the plywood sheet and one leg across the width. Make one leg by cutting an 18-in.-wide, 48-in.-long strip from the short end of the sheet. Then rip-cut another 18-in.-wide strip along the length of the remaining sheet for the other two legs.

2 Lay out the three legs. Follow the *Leg Layout* drawing, page 72, to draw the leg profiles, half-lap notches and round bottom cutouts. Scribe the 4¼-in.-radius cutouts with a compass **(See Photo A).**

3 Cut the three legs to shape with a jig saw: To cut out the square-bottomed half-lap notches, drill

PHOTO A: Lay out the three leg shapes on 18-in.-wide sections of plywood. Draw the curved bottom cutouts that form the bench feet with a compass set to a 4¼-in. radius.

⅜-in.-dia. pilot holes in the corners of the notches first. This will allow room for turning the jig saw at the bottom of the notch. Cut out the notches. Square-off the bottom of each notch with a narrow file and sandpaper.

4 Cut the seat panel to size.

Entry Bench

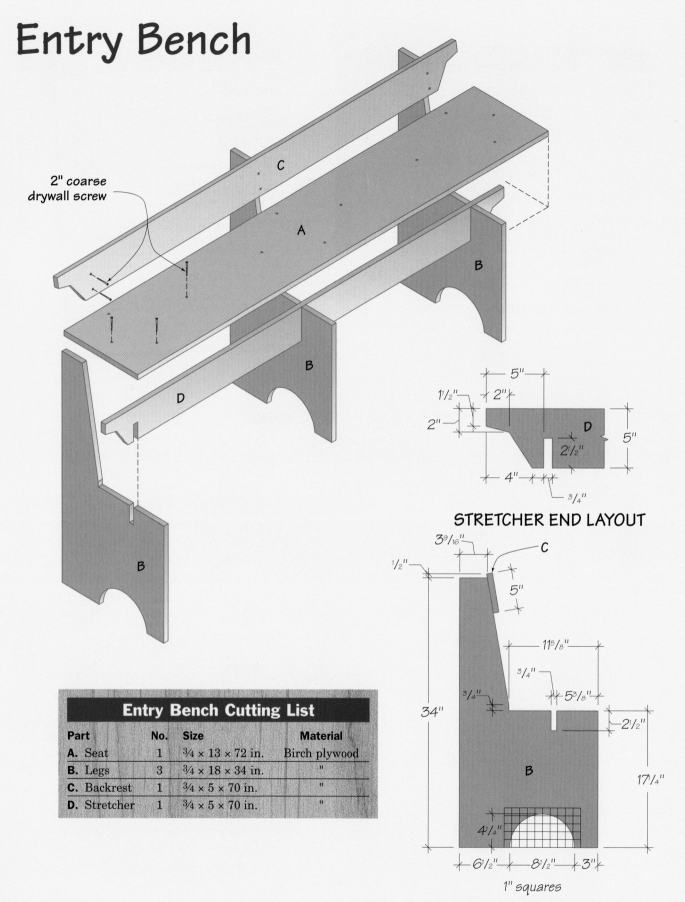

2" coarse drywall screw

C

A

B

B

D

B

STRETCHER END LAYOUT

5"

1 1/2"

2"

2"

D

5"

2 1/2"

4"

3/4"

3 9/16"

1/2"

C

5"

11 5/8"

3/4"

3/4"

5 3/8"

34"

2 1/2"

B

17 1/4"

4 1/4"

6 1/2"

8 1/2"

3"

1" squares

LEG LAYOUT

Entry Bench Cutting List

Part	No.	Size	Material
A. Seat	1	3/4 × 13 × 72 in.	Birch plywood
B. Legs	3	3/4 × 18 × 34 in.	"
C. Backrest	1	3/4 × 5 × 70 in.	"
D. Stretcher	1	3/4 × 5 × 70 in.	"

MAKE THE BACKREST & STRETCHER

5 Cut stretcher and backrest to size.

6 Since the end profiles of the stretcher and backrest match, follow the *Stretcher End Layout* drawing, page 72, to mark the ends of both workpieces with the angled cutting profile. Trim the ends of the parts to shape with a jig saw.

7 Mark the stretcher with three half-lap notches, two spaced 5 in. from the ends and one centered on its length. Cut out the stretcher half-lap notches as you cut the legs, first drilling out clearance holes in the bottom corners of the notches, then removing the waste with a jig saw. File the notch corners square **(See Photo B).**

8 Test-fit the half-lap joints by slipping the stretcher over the bench legs so the notches between the parts interlock **(See Photo C).** You'll know you've got a correct fit if the top edge of the stretcher is flush with the top (seat) edges of the legs. A poor fit can be remedied by either widening or deepening the notches slightly with a file.

ASSEMBLE THE BENCH

9 Spread glue into the half-lap notches on the stretcher and legs and assemble these parts.

10 Set the seat in place on the legs and adjust it so the seat overhangs the ends of the stretcher by 1 in. Mark this position on the bottom face of the seat. Mark stretcher and leg centerlines on the top face of the seat as well, for locating screws. Spread glue on the legs where the seat will go. Reposition the seat on the legs and fasten it in place with 2-in. countersunk drywall screws.

11 Clamp the backrest on the upper ends of the legs so it overhangs 5 in. on each end and ½ in. above the tops of the legs. Mark the backrest for driving pairs of screws at each leg. Spread glue on the edges of the legs in the backrest areas, clamp the backrest in place and fasten it to the legs with 2-in. countersunk drywall screws.

FINISHING TOUCHES

12 Fill recessed screwheads and plywood voids with wood putty and sand the entire bench smooth. Brush or roll on a coat of primer and two coats of paint.

PHOTO B: Cut the three half-lap notches in the stretcher with a jig saw. Drill ⅜-in.-dia. clearance holes in the bottom corners of the notches first, so you can turn the saw to cut the square bottoms.

PHOTO C: Slip the seat and stretcher notches together to check the fit of the half-lap joints. File the notches wider or deeper, a little at a time, to improve the fit, if necessary.

PHOTO D: Install the seat and the backrest on the leg assembly with glue and 2-in. drywall screws, driven into countersunk pilot holes.

Wall-hung Coatrack

Hang coats in style on this Arts-and-Crafts-inspired wall-mounted coatrack. The flat top even provides a place for gloves or keys. We built this rack from red oak, but you could use quartersawn white oak to make the project even more authentically Arts-and-Crafts.

Vital statistics

TYPE: Coatrack

OVERALL SIZE: 32L by 10¾H by 8D

MATERIAL: Red oak

JOINERY: Butt joints reinforced with glue and screws

CONSTRUCTION DETAILS:
- Decorative end profiles duplicated using a full-size pattern
- Screwheads concealed with ⅜-in.-dia. oak plugs

FINISH: Stain and varnish

BUILDING TIME: 3-4 hours

Shopping List

- ☐ (1) 1 × 10 in. × 6 ft. red oak
- ☐ (1) 1 × 6 in. × 6 ft. red oak
- ☐ (4) Coat hooks
- ☐ #8 × 1½-in. flathead wood screws
- ☐ ⅜-in.-dia. oak wood plugs
- ☐ #8 × 2-in. brass screws, finish washers, wall anchors (if necessary)
- ☐ Wood glue
- ☐ Finishing materials

Wall-hung Coatrack: Step-by-step

LAY OUT THE PARTS

❶ Crosscut a 32-in. board from the oak 1 × 10, and rip the board to 8 in. wide to form the coatrack top.

❷ Make the coatrack ends: Crosscut a 21-in. board from the oak 1 × 10 then rip it to 7 in. wide. Crosscut this workpiece to make the coatrack end pieces.

❸ Crosscut a 28½-in. workpiece from the oak 1 × 6, and rip the board to 5 in. wide, forming the coatrack back.

PHOTO A: Lay out the tapered profile on the back panel with a straightedge, and use a full-size paper or cardboard template as a guide for drawing the curved end profiles.

Wall-hung Coatrack

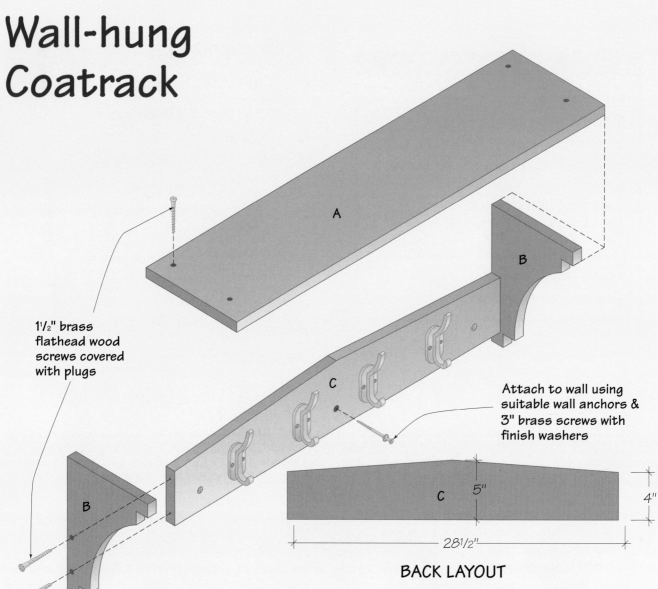

1¹/₂" brass flathead wood screws covered with plugs

A

B

C

B

Attach to wall using suitable wall anchors & 3" brass screws with finish washers

C

5"

4"

28¹/₂"

BACK LAYOUT

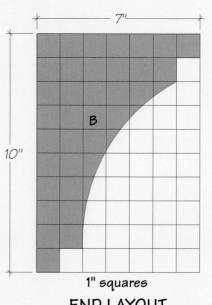

7"

B

10"

1" squares

END LAYOUT

Wall-hung Coatrack Cutting List			
Part	**No.**	**Size**	**Material**
A. Top	1	¾ × 8 × 32 in.	Red oak
B. Ends	2	¾ × 7 × 10 in.	"
C. Back	1	¾ × 5 × 28½ in.	"

PHOTO B: Fasten the coatrack ends to the back with glue and flathead wood screws driven into counterbored pilot holes. Clamp the parts together first to hold them securely while you install the screws.

④ Draw the back profile: Make a mark 14¼ in. along one edge of the back workpiece to locate the widest point of the back profile. Refer to the *Back Layout* drawing, page 76, to draw the two tapering lines from this point out to the ends of the back panel.

⑤ Enlarge the *End Layout* grid drawing, page 76, to form a full-size paper or cardboard pattern of the coatrack end profile. Cut out the pattern and use it as a template for drawing profiles on both coatrack end workpieces **(See Photo A).**

CUT OUT THE PARTS

⑥ Cut the back profile using a jig saw or circular saw. Make these straight cuts with your saw guided against a straightedge.

⑦ Cut the coatrack ends to shape: Clamp each end to your worksurface, providing sufficient clear space beneath the workpiece for the saw blade. Install a narrow, fine-toothed blade in your jig saw and cut out the end profiles. TIP: *If your jig saw has various settings for adjusting blade orbit, set the saw for no orbiting action to minimize tearout while you cut.*

ASSEMBLE THE COATRACK

⑧ Fasten the coatrack ends to the back: Arrange the parts so the back will be flush with the long edges of the ends and inset 1 in. up from the bottoms of the ends. The profiled edge of the back should face up. Drill two counterbored pilot holes through each coatrack end and into the ends of the back panel for screws using a bit that bores a ⅜-in.-dia. counterbore. Spread glue on the ends of the back panel, set the ends and back together and attach the parts with 1½-in. brass flathead wood screws **(See Photo B).**

⑨ Install the top. First, clamp the coatrack assembly in a bench vise to hold it securely while you attach the top. Set the top in place on the coatrack ends so the back edges of the parts are flush and a 1-in. overhang is provided around the ends and front. Mark the top to indicate centerlines of the end pieces for locating pairs of attachment screws. NOTE: *Be sure to position the front screws far enough in on the end pieces so the screws won't pierce the notched cutouts.* Drill pilot holes with ⅜-in.-dia. counterbores through the top and into each coatrack end at the screw locations. Spread glue on the top edges of the ends. Fasten the

PHOTO C: Once you've attached the coatrack parts, cover the screw-heads with face-grain red oak plugs held in place with glue. Tap each plug into its counterbore with a wooden mallet.

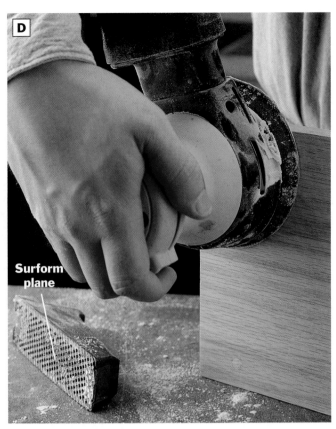

Surform plane

PHOTO D: Shave the plugs so they're nearly flush with the surrounding wood surface using a Surform plane or a wood rasp. Sand away the remaining waste with coarse sandpaper.

PHOTO E: Brush or wipe on a coat of wood stain with a foam brush or clean rag, then wipe off the excess stain before it dries. Wear disposable gloves to protect your hands. Topcoat the project with varnish.

top to the ends with #8 × 1½-in. brass flathead wood screws.

INSTALL WOOD PLUGS

⑩ Squeeze a drop of glue into each screwhead counterbore, and tap in oak wood plugs with a wooden mallet to conceal the screws **(See Photo C)**.

⑪ Use a Surform plane or wood rasp and file to trim the wood plugs down until they are nearly flush with the surrounding wood surface. Sand the plugs flush with 80-grit sandpaper **(See Photo D)**.

FINISHING TOUCHES

⑫ Sand all project surfaces with 150-, then 220-grit sandpaper until smooth. Hand-sand the coatrack end profiles as well to remove any saw marks.

⑬ Brush or wipe on several coats

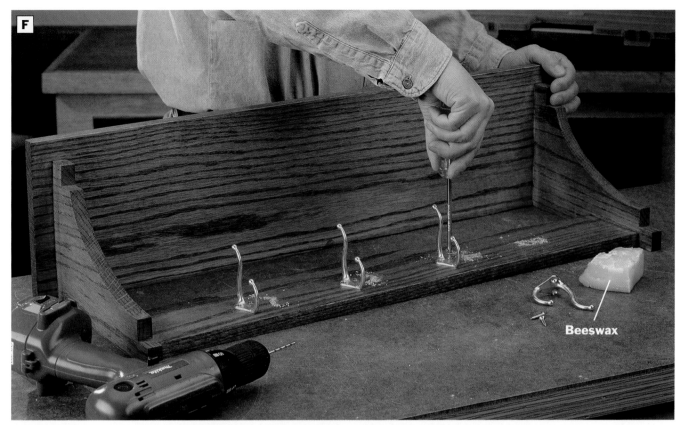

PHOTO F: Lay out and attach four coat hooks to the coatrack back. Drill pilot holes for the screws, especially if the screws are made of brass. Space the hooks about 6 in. apart. TIP: *Coat the screw threads with beeswax to make them easier to drive into the oak.*

of wood stain, and wipe off the excess stain before it dries **(See Photo E).** Protect the project with two coats of varnish.

⓮ Lay out and install the coat hooks: Arrange the four hooks so they're spaced about 6 in. apart and centered vertically on the coatrack back. Drill pilot holes for the attachment screws, and fasten the hooks using the screws provided with the hooks **(See Photo F).**

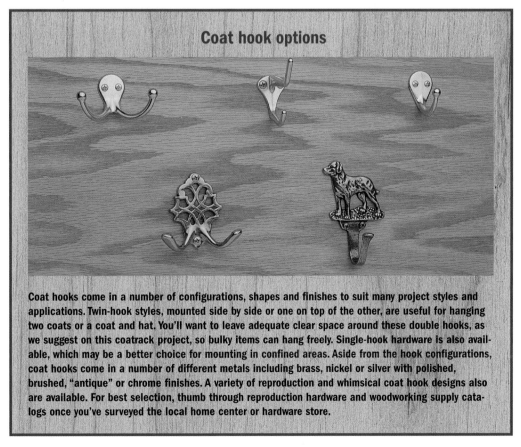

Coat hook options

Coat hooks come in a number of configurations, shapes and finishes to suit many project styles and applications. Twin-hook styles, mounted side by side or one on top of the other, are useful for hanging two coats or a coat and hat. You'll want to leave adequate clear space around these double hooks, as we suggest on this coatrack project, so bulky items can hang freely. Single-hook hardware is also available, which may be a better choice for mounting in confined areas. Aside from the hook configurations, coat hooks come in a number of different metals including brass, nickel or silver with polished, brushed, "antique" or chrome finishes. A variety of reproduction and whimsical coat hook designs also are available. For best selection, thumb through reproduction hardware and woodworking supply catalogs once you've surveyed the local home center or hardware store.

Schoolhouse Desk

Long before there were classrooms equipped with computers and Internet access, there were one-room schoolhouses outfitted with a chalkboard and rows of single-unit desks. These desks recall a simpler era when children needed a sturdy surface on which to practice their reading, writing and arithmetic. Today, a desk like this still functions for doing schoolwork at home, but kids will also find it the perfect place to color, draw or paint. There's even a shelf below the desktop to store their supplies. Best of all, the whole project is made from a single sheet of 4 × 8 plywood.

Schoolhouse Desk: Step-by-step

LAY OUT & CUT THE PARTS

❶ Refer to the *Cutting List* on page 82 to lay out the project parts on the plywood sheet. Creating a cutting diagram now will economize your cutting and help to minimize waste. Mark each project part with the letter that corresponds to the *Cutting List,* to help you identify the parts once they're cut.

❷ Cut the parts to size. Support the plywood on sawhorses while you cut out the parts with a circular saw. Guide your cuts with a

PHOTO A: Draw a cutting diagram on the plywood sheet to lay out the project parts. Mark each part with a letter that corresponds to the *Cutting List* on page 82 to help identify them. Clamp a straightedge in place to guide the saw as you cut the parts to size.

Schoolhouse Desk

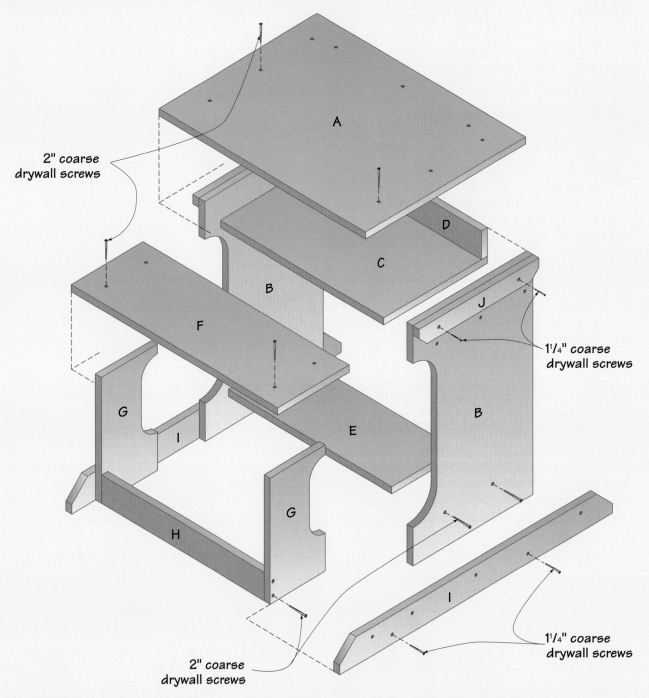

2" coarse
drywall screws

A

D

C

B

J

1¼" coarse
drywall screws

F

B

G

E

I

G

H

I

1¼" coarse
drywall screws

2" coarse
drywall screws

Schoolhouse Desk Cutting List

Part	No.	Size	Material	Part	No.	Size	Material
A. Desktop	1	¾ × 20 × 26 in.	Birch plywood	**F.** Bench seat	1	¾ × 9 × 26 in.	Birch plywood
B. Desk legs	2	¾ × 15 × 25¼ in.	"	**G.** Bench legs	2	¾ × 7 × 13¼ in.	"
C. Shelf	1	¾ × 13× 20½ in.	"	**H.** Bench stretcher	1	¾ × 3 × 20½ in.	"
D. Shelf back	1	¾ × 3 × 20½ in.	"	**I.** Runners	2	¾ × 3 × 34 in.	"
E. Footrest	1	¾ × 8 × 20½ in.	"	**J.** Desktop cleats	2	¾ × 2 × 15 in.	"

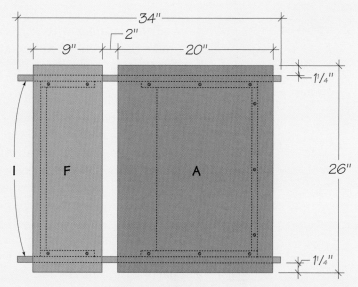

PLAN VIEW

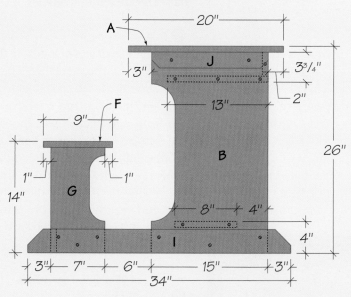

SIDE ELEVATION

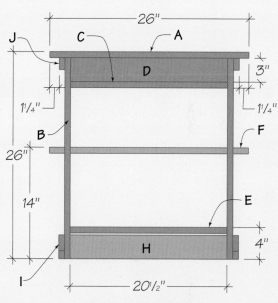

FRONT ELEVATION

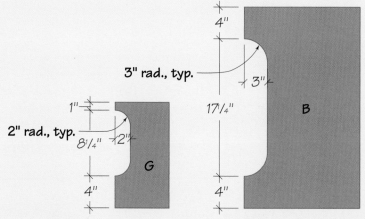

BENCH LEG LAYOUT   **DESK LEG LAYOUT**

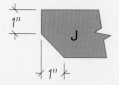

TOP CLEAT END LAYOUT

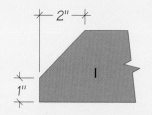

RUNNER END LAYOUT

PHOTO B: Lay out the curves on the bench legs. Set your compass to draw a 2-in. radius to draw the arcs. Connect the layout lines with a straightedge.

straightedge clamped to the plywood so the saw follows the layout lines accurately. Make the longest cuts first to break the plywood sheet into more manageable portions (**See Photo A**).

BUILD THE BENCH
❸ Make the bench legs: Refer to the *Bench Leg Layout* drawing,

page 83, to draw curved cutouts along one long edge of each bench leg. Scribe the curves with a compass set to draw a 2-in. radius. Connect the curves with a straightedge (**See Photo B**).

❹ Cut the bench legs to shape: Secure each workpiece with clamps to your worksurface to

hold it while you cut, and follow your layout lines with a jig saw to make the bench leg cutouts (**See Photo C**).

❺ Assemble the legs and bench stretcher: See the *Exploded View* drawing, page 82, for information on arranging the bench stretcher between the two bench legs. Notice that the stretcher aligns with the back bottom corner of the legs. Spread glue on the ends of the stretcher, clamp it in place between the legs and attach the parts with countersunk 2-in. drywall screws driven through the legs and into the stretcher.

❻ Install the bench seat: Position the bench seat on the ends of the legs opposite the stretcher. The seat should overhang the legs 2 in. on the sides and 1 in. over the front and back edges. Lay out leg centerlines for screws on the top face of the seat. Drill countersunk pilot holes along these lines, apply glue to the top ends of the legs and secure the seat to the legs with 2-in. drywall screws (**See Photo D**).

ASSEMBLE THE DESK
❼ Attach the shelf back to the shelf: Orient the parts so one long edge of the shelf overlaps the shelf back, forming an "L" shape. Spread glue on the mating surfaces of these parts and clamp them facedown on your workbench so the clamps overhang the bench. Drill countersunk pilot holes through the shelf and into the shelf back. Fasten the parts with 2-in. drywall screws (**See Photo E**).

❽ Mark and cut the curved cutouts in the desk legs, according to the *Desk Leg Layout* drawing, page 83. To draw the shape, scribe

PHOTO C: Clamp each bench leg to your workbench and cut to shape with a jig saw. Be sure your clamps don't interfere with the path of the saw.

the 3-in.-radius curves with a compass, and connect the curves with a straight line. Make the cutouts with a jig saw.

❾ Mark both faces of the desk legs to determine where they will attach to the shelf, shelf back and footrest. The *Side* and *Front Elevation* drawings on page 83 show the locations of these parts. Draw part outlines as well as screw locations on the legs **(See Photo F).**

❿ Attach the shelf assembly to the desk legs: Arrange the parts upside down on your workbench. This will ensure that the top edge of the shelf back and the top of the legs will be flush. It's helpful to place a couple 3-in.-wide scrap blocks under the front edge of the shelf for support. Spread glue on the ends of the shelf assembly and secure the shelf between the legs with a clamp or two. Attach the legs to the shelf and shelf back with 2-in. drywall screws, driving the fasteners at the marked screw locations.

⓫ Attach the footrest to the desk legs: Spread glue on the ends of the footrest and align it with the marks on the insides of the legs. Support the footrest with 3¼-in.-wide scraps of wood from beneath and clamp it in place. Drive countersunk 2-in. screws through the legs and into the footrest **(See Photo G).**

⓬ Position the desktop on the desk legs, and mark it for installation: Set the desktop on the legs so it overhangs the legs 2 in. on the back and sides but 3 in. on the front. Outline the shapes of the legs and shelf back on the top and bottom faces of

PHOTO D: After the bench stretcher is secured between the legs, fasten the bench seat with glue and countersunk 2-in. drywall screws.

PHOTO E: Spread glue along one edge of the shelf back and clamp it flush with the back edge of the shelf. Attach the parts with countersunk 2-in. drywall screws.

PHOTO F: Lay out the shelf and footrest positions on both sides of both desk legs. See the *Side Elevation* drawing, page 83, to position these parts.

PHOTO G: Install the footrest with glue and screws. Insert a couple of 3¼-in.-wide spacer blocks beneath the footrest to hold it in position temporarily while you screw it in place.

PHOTO H: Install the desktop on the legs and shelf back with glue and countersunk 2-in. drywall screws. Mark the positions of the legs and shelf back on the desktop for locating the screws.

PHOTO I: Mark the angled ends of the runners and cut the corners with a circular saw. Support your straightedge from beneath with a wood scrap clamped to the workbench.

the desktop with a pencil and straightedge to determine the screwhole positions.

⓭ Attach the desktop: Move the project to the shop floor so you can work at a comfortable height. Spread glue on the top edges of the legs and shelf back, and set the desktop in position. Hold the desktop steady while you drill countersunk pilot holes for the screws. Secure the top with 2-in. drywall screws (**See Photo H**).

⓮ Mark and cut the angled corners on the desktop cleats and runners to match the *Top Cleat* and *Runner End Layout* drawings, page 83 (**See Photo I**). Guide the saw against a clamped straightedge. Because of the narrow width of these cleats and runners, you may need to support the straightedge with a piece of scrap before making the cuts.

FINISHING TOUCHES

⓯ Fill all the screwholes and any edge voids in the bench and desk. Sand the bench, desk, top cleats and runners smooth (**See Photo J**).

⓰ Prepare all project surfaces for paint with a coat of primer.

PHOTO J: Once you've filled all the screwholes and any voids in the plywood, sand the bench and desk before you prime and paint. A random-orbit sander and 150-grit sandpaper will make this a quick task.

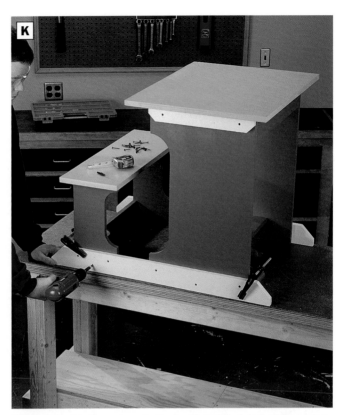

PHOTO K: Fasten the runners to the bench and desk legs with countersunk 1¼-in. drywall screws. Hold the parts together with clamps while you drive the screws. Stagger the screw pattern.

⓱ Determine the paint scheme for your desk. If you choose multiple colors, mask off the necessary areas with tape and apply one color at a time. Be sure that each color has dried completely before taping it off and painting another area.

⓲ Fasten the desktop cleats to the desk legs: Clamp the cleats in place so their angled corners face down. Drill countersunk pilot holes through the cleats and into the legs. Install the cleats with a couple of 1¼-in. drywall screws.

⓳ Attach the runners to the bench and desk: Clamp the runners along the bottom ends of the bench and desk legs so the angled ends of the runners face up. Position the parts so the ends of the runners overhang the bench and desk by 3 in. (See the *Side Elevation* drawing, page 83). Drive a staggered row of 1¼-in. drywall screws through the runners to fasten the parts together **(See Photo K).**

⓴ Fill the screwhead holes in the desktop cleats and runners with wood putty and sand smooth. Touch up these spots with paint to complete the project **(See Photo L).**

PHOTO L: Conceal the screwheads on the desktop cleats and runners with wood putty and paint.

Lap-joint Picture Frame

Add the crowning touch to a cherished family photo when you display it in a picture frame you've built yourself. This frame design features half-lap joints in the corners—a simple and attractive way to join the four frame pieces together. Build the frame from one wood type or combine a couple of contrasting species, like walnut and maple. You could even build a frame from plywood or particleboard and paint it. The choice is up to you.

Lap-joint Picture Frame: Step-by-step

MAKE THE LONG & SHORT FRAME PIECES

❶ Crosscut the short and long frame pieces to length.

❷ Rout the half laps: Since the half-lap depth and width matches on all four frame members, it's possible to gang-rout like-frame pieces using a simple router setup. Cut the short frame half laps first. Install a ¾-in. straight bit in your router, and set the cutting depth to ⅜ in. Lay out the 1½-in.-wide lap joints across both short frames with the ends of the parts aligned. Then clamp the short frame pieces together between two ¾-in.-thick scrap strips. The scraps will serve as backers to keep the router bit from tearing out the wood as it exits the half-lap cuts. Clamp a straight-edged piece of scrap over the short frame assembly, positioned so the router bit will cut along one set of half-lap layout lines. Mill half the

PHOTO A: Gang-rout the half-lap joints in the short frame pieces, then the long frame pieces. Clamp pairs of frame pieces between two scraps to back up the router cuts, and guide the router against a straightedge. Mill the half laps in two router passes.

lap-joint area, cutting across both the scrap and the short frame workpieces in one pass. Loosen the clamps, reposition the short frames to align the router for cutting away the remaining waste, reclamp and make another pass to complete one set of lap cuts. Turn the frame workpieces end-for-end in the router setup to rout half laps on the other ends of the parts **(See Photo A)**.

Lap-joint Picture Frame

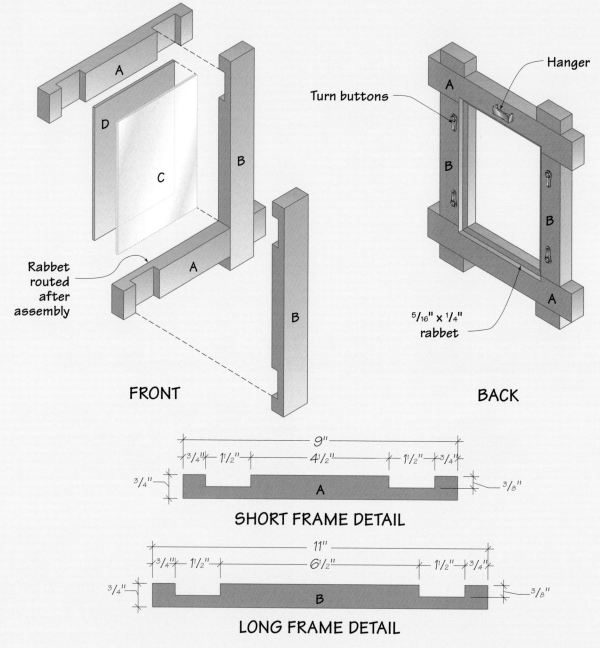

Hanger

Turn buttons

FRONT

BACK

Rabbet routed after assembly

$^5/_{16}"$ x $^1/_4"$ rabbet

SHORT FRAME DETAIL

9"

$^3/_4"$ 1$^1/_2"$ 4$^1/_2"$ 1$^1/_2"$ $^3/_4"$

$^3/_4"$ A $^3/_8"$

LONG FRAME DETAIL

11"

$^3/_4"$ 1$^1/_2"$ 6$^1/_2"$ 1$^1/_2"$ $^3/_4"$

$^3/_4"$ B $^3/_8"$

RABBET DETAIL

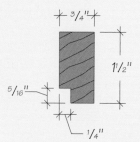

$^3/_4"$

1$^1/_2"$

$^5/_{16}"$

$^1/_4"$

Lap-joint Picture Frame Cutting List			
Part	**No.**	**Size**	**Material**
A. Short frames	2	$^3/_4 \times 1^1/_2 \times 9$ in.	Any wood
B. Long frames	2	$^3/_4 \times 1^1/_2 \times 11$ in.	"
C. Glass	1	$^1/_8 \times 5 \times 7$ in.	
D. Backer	1	$^1/_8 \times 5 \times 7$ in.	Hardboard

③ Rout the half-lap joints on the long frame pieces using the same router setup and procedure as you used in Step 2.

ASSEMBLE THE FRAME

④ Dry-assemble the long and short frame pieces to check the fit of the lap joints. Sand the routed areas slightly wider or deeper to improve the fit.

⑤ Spread glue into the routed areas, and clamp the frame parts together **(See Photo B)**.

⑥ Rout a rabbeted recess around the inside back edges of the frame for housing the glass, photo and backer. Use a piloted ¼-in. rabbeting bit set to a depth of ⁵⁄₁₆ to mill this rabbet **(See Photo C)**.

⑦ Square up the corners of the back rabbet with a sharp chisel.

FINISHING TOUCHES

⑧ Sand the frame with 150-, then 220-grit sandpaper, and apply your choice of finish.

⑨ Fasten four turn buttons around the rabbeted area on the back of the frame to hold the glass, photo and backer in place.

⑩ Insert the glass, photo and backer in the frame, and swivel the turn buttons into position.

⑪ Carefully tack a sawtooth picture hanger to the top short frame piece on the frame back **(See Photo D)**. You may want to remove the glass, photo and backer first.

PHOTO B: Spread glue in the lap-joint cutouts and clamp the frame pieces together.

PHOTO C: Rout a ¼-in.-wide, ⁵⁄₁₆-in.-deep rabbet around the inside back edge of the frame for the glass, photo and backer. Square up the corners of the rabbet with a chisel.

PHOTO D: Install turn buttons and a sawtooth picture hanger on the back of the frame.

Building other frame sizes

The picture frame depicted in the technical drawings, these photos and in the *Cutting List* is sized for a 5 × 7-in. photograph. If you'd like to make similar frames for other popular photo sizes, build according to the part dimensions listed below:

For 4 × 6-in. photographs:
Short frame pieces: ¾ × 1½ × 8 in.
Long frame pieces: ¾ × 1½ × 10 in.
Glass, backer: ⅛ × 4 × 6 in.

For 8 × 10-in. photographs:
Short frame pieces: ¾ × 1½ × 12 in.
Long frame pieces: ¾ × 1½ × 14 in.
Glass, backer: ⅛ × 8 × 10 in.

Basic Bookcase

Good-quality prefabricated bookcases are tough to come by for less than $100. Spend a fraction of that amount on materials for this project, and you can construct a bookcase that will last for years. Our low-standing bookcase is just the right height for kids, but it's also a sturdy and practical addition to any room in the house. Build it from one sheet of paint-grade plywood in an afternoon.

Basic Bookcase: Step-by-step

CUT THE PARTS

❶ Rip and crosscut the bookcase back and top to size.

❷ Rip a 10-in.-wide, 62⅝-in. strip of plywood, then crosscut the strip in half to form the two bookcase sides.

❸ Lay out the three shelves end-for-end along one long edge of the plywood sheet, then cut off this strip of shelving. Crosscut the strip along your reference lines to divide it into three shelves (**See Photo A**).

PHOTO A: Lay out the bookcase parts on the plywood sheet, then rip and crosscut them to size. We arranged the shelves end-to-end on the plywood so we could rip one long strip, then crosscut the strip twice to form the three shelves.

Basic Bookcase

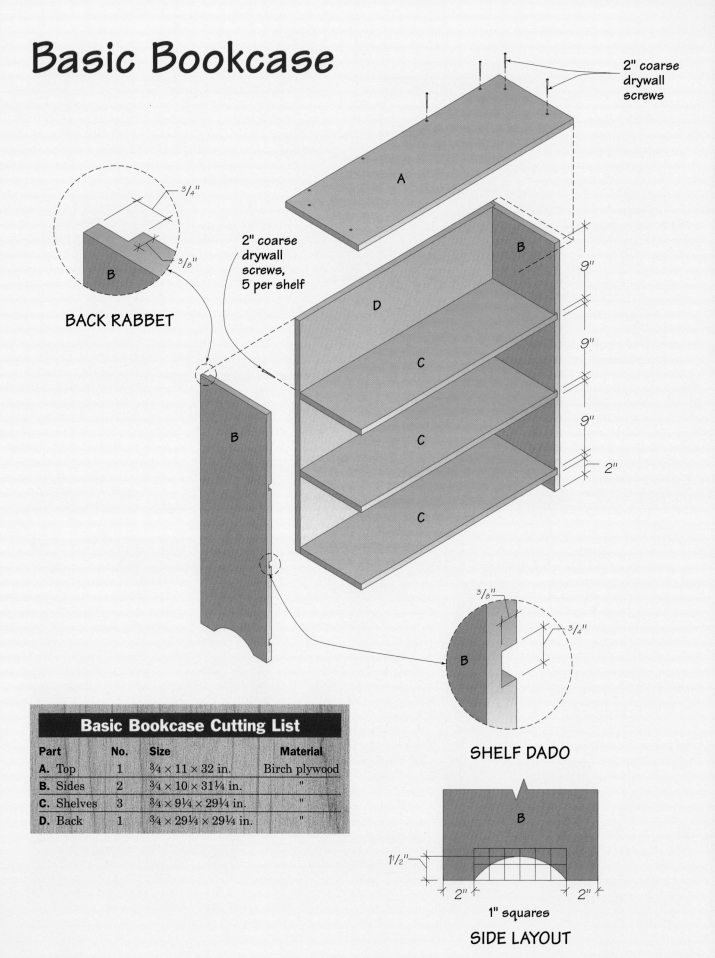

BACK RABBET

3/4"

3/8"

B

2" coarse drywall screws

2" coarse drywall screws, 5 per shelf

A

B

D

C

C

C

9"

9"

9"

2"

B

B

SHELF DADO

3/8"

3/4"

B

SIDE LAYOUT

1 1/2"

2"

2"

1" squares

Basic Bookcase Cutting List

Part	No.	Size	Material
A. Top	1	3/4 × 11 × 32 in.	Birch plywood
B. Sides	2	3/4 × 10 × 31¼ in.	"
C. Shelves	3	3/4 × 9¼ × 29¼ in.	"
D. Back	1	3/4 × 29¼ × 29¼ in.	"

Make the sides

4 Draw and cut the arched profiles along the bottom edges of the side panels: Lay out the arches, following the *Side Layout* grid drawing, page 94. Make these curved cuts with a jig saw, and smooth the cut edges with a file and sandpaper.

5 Rout the shelf dadoes in the sides. To set up for this milling operation, clamp the side panels together side by side, so the parts are aligned and configured with the arched ends next to one another. Refer to the *Exploded View* drawing, page 94, to mark the shelf dado locations across both side panels. Rout each shelf dado with a ¾-in.-dia. straight bit set to a depth of ⅜ in. Guide the router base against a straight-edge clamped across the work-pieces, and gang-rout the dadoes across both side panels **(See Photo B)**.

6 Mill rabbets along the inside back edge of each side panel for the bookcase back. Use the same router bit and depth setting as for the shelf dadoes (See the *Back Rabbet* detail drawing, page 94). Clamp a straightedge lengthwise along each side panel to guide the router base while you cut each rabbet **(See Photo C)**.

Assemble the bookcase

7 Dry-fit the shelves and back panel in the bookcase sides to be sure the parts fit in the dado and rabbet grooves. NOTE: *Some plywood is slightly thicker than ¾ in., so the shelves may fit tightly in the dado grooves. If this is true for your plywood, widen the dadoes slightly with a file until the shelves fit without force.*

PHOTO B: Clamp the sides together side by side, lay out the shelf dado locations and gang-rout the dadoes across both sides. Clamp a straightedge across the side workpieces to guide the router cuts.

PHOTO C: Rout ¾-in.-wide, ⅜-in.-deep rabbets along the inside back edge of each side panel for the bookcase back. Clamp each side panel to your bench to hold it securely as you rout the rabbet, and guide the router base against a straightedge.

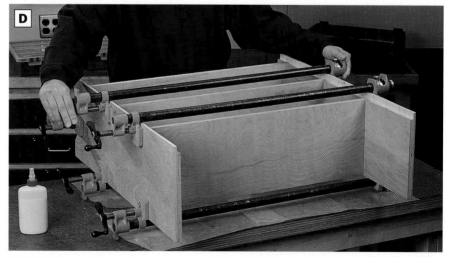

PHOTO D: Glue and clamp the shelves into their dadoes in the bookcase sides. Keep the shelves flush with the front edges of the sides so they don't obstruct the back rabbets.

PHOTO E: Install the back on the bookcase with glue and screws driven into the back edges of the shelves. Mark the shelf locations on the back first, so you can drive the screws accurately.

PHOTO F: Position the top panel on the bookcase and fasten it with 2-in. drywall screws driven into countersunk pilot holes.

8 Assemble the shelves and sides: Spread glue in the dadoes, set the shelves in place and clamp up the parts. Be sure the shelves are flush with the front edges of the bookcase sides (**See Photo D**).

9 Install the back. First, mark shelf centerlines across the back panel for installing screws. Then spread glue in the rabbets and set the back in place so the top edges of the sides and back are flush. Drive countersunk 2-in. drywall screws through the back and into the shelves along your pencil reference lines (**See Photo E**).

10 Attach the top: Set the top in place on the bookcase so the back edge is flush with the bookcase back. The ends and front should overhang evenly. Mark centerlines on the top for driving screws into the sides and back. Drill countersunk pilot holes along these lines. Fasten the top in place with 2-in. drywall screws (**See Photo F**).

FINISHING TOUCHES
11 Fill the screwhead recesses, gaps around the shelf dadoes and any voids in the plywood with wood putty (**See Photo G**).

12 Sand the puttied areas and all project surfaces smooth with 150-grit sandpaper.

13 Finish the bookshelf by rolling or brushing on a coat of primer followed by two coats of paint (**See Photo H**).

PHOTO G: Conceal the screwheads and any voids or gaps in the plywood with wood putty. Sand the putty smooth when it dries.

PHOTO H: Roll or brush on a coat of primer to all exposed surfaces, followed by two coats of paint.

Stiffening long shelves

The main factor that determines the width of a bookcase is the load-bearing capacity of the shelves. A ¾-in.-thick plywood shelf can span about 30 in. without additional support before it begins to sag. If you decide to modify this bookcase project and build it with longer shelves, stiffen each shelf by gluing and nailing a 1½-in.-wide strip of solid wood or plywood along the front edge. You could also double-up the thickness of the shelves by gluing on another layer of ¾-in.-thick plywood. A third, but more involved alternative would be to add a vertical divider at the middle of each shelf.

Heavy-duty Sandbox

Here's a sandbox that offers ample seating for young and young-at-heart alike. Made of pressure-treated plywood, this box will weather many years of backyard fun. We've designed it with a solid bottom to keep weed growth at bay as well as two built-in seats on each end. The 16 square-foot sand pit provides plenty of room for constructing imaginary roads or pretend battle sites.

Vital statistics

TYPE: Sandbox

OVERALL SIZE: 72L by 12¾H by 48D

MATERIAL: Pressure-treated plywood

JOINERY: Butt joints reinforced with screws

CONSTRUCTION DETAILS:

· Create a cutting diagram for all the parts on the plywood sheets before you begin cutting

· Drain holes drilled with a 2-in.-dia. hole cutter

FINISH: Primer and paint

BUILDING TIME: 2-3 hours

Shopping List

☐ (2) ¾ in. × 4 × 8 ft. pressure-treated plywood

☐ 2-in. deck screws

☐ Moisture-resistant wood glue

☐ Finishing materials

☐ Screened play sand (about 8 cu. ft.)

Heavy-duty Sandbox: Step-by-step

LAY OUT & CUT THE PARTS
In order to build this project from only two sheets of plywood, it's important to first lay out all the parts before you begin cutting.

❶ Follow the *Plywood Cutting Patterns* drawing on page 100 to measure and mark all of the sandbox parts on the plywood sheets.

❷ Cut the parts to size, following your layout lines. Make the long cuts first, to size the plywood sheets down into more manageable pieces **(See Photo A).**

PHOTO A: Lay out all of the project parts on both sheets of plywood to minimize waste, then cut the parts to size along your layout lines. A long straightedge clamped in place helps ensure accurate saw cuts. When machining pressure-treated wood products, wear a dust mask and work gloves.

Heavy-duty Sandbox

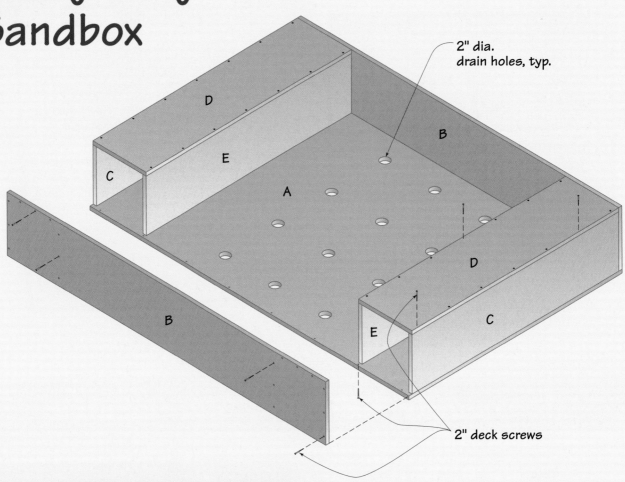

2" dia.
drain holes, typ.
D
B
E
C
A
D
C
E
B
2" deck screws

Heavy-duty Sandbox Cutting List

Part	No.	Size	Material
A. Bottom	1	¾ × 48 × 72 in.	Pressure-treated plywood
B. Front/back	2	¾ × 12 × 72 in.	"
C. Ends	2	¾ × 11¼ × 46½ in.	"
D. Seats	2	¾ × 12 × 46½ in.	"
E. Seat supports	2	¾ × 11¼ × 46½ in.	"

E
E
A
Scrap
C
D
B
B
C
D

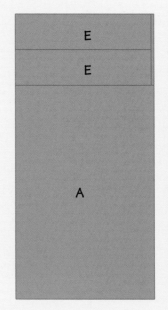

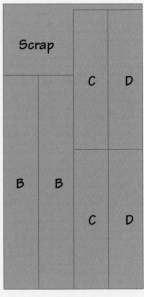

PLYWOOD CUTTING PATTERNS

3 Drill a series of drain holes in the sandbox bottom panel. Locate the holes starting 2 ft. in from the ends of the bottom and 6 in. in from the edges. We marked a grid of 12 holes (three rows of four holes) before drilling, then bored the holes with a corded drill and 2-in. hole saw **(See Photo B)**. If you decide to drill smaller-diameter holes, drill more than 12 in all to provide adequate drainage.

Assemble the sandbox

4 Install the sandbox end panels on the bottom panel: Spread moisture-resistant wood glue on the bottom edges of the end panels, and arrange them on the bottom so the outside faces of the ends are flush with the ends of the bottom. Drive countersunk 2-in. deck screws up through the bottom panel to secure the parts.

5 Fasten the seat supports to the bottom panel: Draw reference lines across the bottom panel 12 in. in from the ends of the bottom to mark the seat support locations. Attach the seat supports to the bottom with glue and countersunk deck screws.

6 Attach the seats: Spread glue along the top edges of the end panels and seat supports. Install the seats on the ends and the seat supports with countersunk 2-in. galvanized deck screws.

7 Attach the front and back panels to the sandbox assembly with glue and countersunk deck screws **(See Photo C)**.

8 Finish the sandbox: Sand the entire project smooth, and ease all sharp corners and edges. Topcoat the sandbox with primer and two coats of paint **(See Photo D)**.

PHOTO B: Mark and drill drainage holes in the sandbox bottom panel with a 2-in. hole saw. We drilled a dozen holes 1 ft. apart, spaced 2 ft. in from the ends of the panel.

PHOTO C: After you've assembled the seats on the bottom panel, glue and screw the front and back in place so they cover the ends of the seats and the edges of the bottom panel.

PHOTO D: Protect the sandbox from the elements and improve its appearance by topcoating with exterior primer and two coats of paint.

Heavy-duty Sandbox **101**

Easy-clean Birdhouse

You'll think the birds are singing your praises when a couple of feathered friends take up residence in this project. Our cedar birdhouse is easy to build, and a hinged panel on the side makes it a snap to clean out for next season once the birds fly south.

Easy-clean Birdhouse: Step-by-step

MAKE THE HOUSE PARTS

❶ Cut the bottom, front, back, side and door to length.

❷ Crosscut a 5¾-in.-long blank for the door stop, then rip-cut the stop to its 2-in. width.

❸ Label the parts with strips of masking tape and their *Cutting List* letter labels to identify them.

❹ Mark the roof angles on the front and back workpieces **(See Photo A).** Cut the roof angles.

❺ Drill the drain holes in the bottom: Mark the bottom for four drain holes, spaced 1½ in. in from the ends and the edges of the bot-

PHOTO A: Cut workpieces for the front, back, bottom, side and door stop. Label the parts so you won't confuse them. Lay out the roof angles on the front and back, and cut out the roof profile on these parts with a jig saw.

Easy-clean Birdhouse

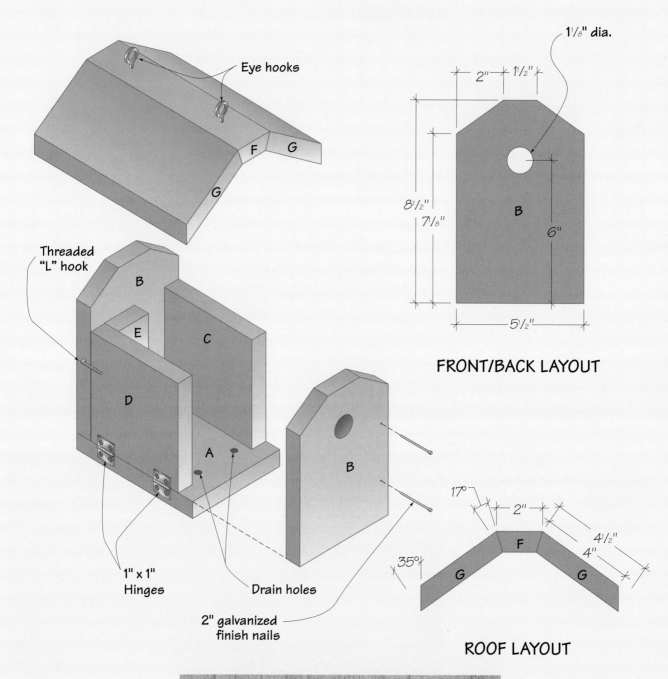

Eye hooks

1⅛" dia.

2" 1½"

8½"
7⅞"

6"

B

5½"

FRONT/BACK LAYOUT

Threaded
"L" hook

B

E

C

D

A

B

1" x 1"
Hinges

Drain holes

2" galvanized
finish nails

17°

2"

4½"

4"

F

G   G

35°

ROOF LAYOUT

Easy-clean Birdhouse Cutting List

Part	No.	Size	Material
A. Bottom	1	⅞ × 5½ × 7 in.	Cedar
B. Front/back	2	⅞ × 5½ × 8½ in.	"
C. Side	1	⅞ × 5½ × 5¾ in.	"
D. Door	1	⅞ × 5½ × 5¾ in.	"
E. Door stop	1	⅞ × 2 × 5¾ in.	"
F. Roof peak	1	⅞ × 2 × 9½ in.	"
G. Roof sections	2	⅞ × 4½ × 9½ in.	"

tom panel. Bore the holes with a ⅜-in.-dia. drill bit.

6 Drill the bird entry hole in the front panel: Mark the centerpoint of the entry hole 6 in. up from the bottom of the front panel, centered on the width of the workpiece. Drill the hole with a spade bit (**See Photo B**). NOTE: *See the tint box, below, for entry hole sizes that are appropriate for specific kinds of birds.*

ASSEMBLE THE HOUSE

7 Arrange the front, back, side and bottom together so the house is upside down on your worksurface. Check the fit of the parts. The bottom panel overlaps the bottom ends of the front, back and side. The side fits in between the front and back.

8 Spread moisture-resistant glue on the mating surfaces of the parts, and clamp them together in the same orientation as Step 7. Slip the door in place without glue so it can serve as a spacer. Reinforce the glue joints with 2-in. galvanized finish nails, but do not nail into the door (**See Photo C**).

9 Install the door. First, check the fit of the door on the house assembly. If it fits so tightly that it binds against the front and back panels, sand the door edges until it moves freely in its opening. Otherwise the wood may swell once it's exposed to the elements and the door may not open. Fasten the door to the house bottom with two hinges, spaced about ½ in. in from the edges of the door (**See Photo D**).

10 Glue the door stop to the birdhouse back so it is flush against the back of the door.

PHOTO B: Mark the centerpoint of the bird access hole on the birdhouse front, and drill the hole with a spade bit. Clamp a backer board beneath the bird house front before you drill the hole to keep the bit from tearing out as it exits.

PHOTO C: Assemble the front, back, side and bottom with glue and clamps. Insert the door (without glue) to serve as a spacer. Nail the glued parts together and recess the nailheads.

Suggested entry hole sizes by species

The size of the entry hole you drill on your birdhouse will influence the species of birds that may take up residence there. Here are some recommended hole sizes for attracting different birds:

1⅛-in. hole
Chickadee, Prothonotary Warbler

1¼-in. hole
Titmouse, Red-breasted Nuthatch, Downy Woodpecker, House Wren

1⅜-in. hole
White-breasted Nuthatch, Tree & Violet-Green Swallows

PHOTO D: Attach the door to the birdhouse bottom with two hinges. Mark pilot holes for the hinge screws first with a scratch awl.

BUILD & INSTALL THE ROOF

⑪ Make the roof peak: Crosscut a 9½-in.-long section of 1 × 6 first, so you'll have ample extra material for supporting the saw base when you cut the narrow peak to width. Lay out the long beveled edges of the peak so they taper from 2 in. on its top face to 1½ in. on its bottom face.

⑫ Bevel-rip the peak to shape with a jig saw: Set a bevel gauge to match the peak bevel angles, and use the gauge to adjust the saw base and blade to the same angle **(See Photo E).** Cut the peak bevels.

⑬ Crosscut two boards for the roof sections: Lay out the beveled edges of each roof section according to the angles given in the *Roof Layout* drawing, page 104. Use a protractor to determine and mark the 17° and 35° beveled edges on the roof section boards, then set the saw base accordingly to bevel-rip the edges **(See Photo F).**

⑭ Dry-fit the roof parts on the birdhouse to check the fit of the bevel joints. Sand or file the beveled edges to improve the fit and close the joints.

PHOTO E: Transfer bevel angles you've marked on the roof parts to your jig saw for setting up the cuts. A bevel gauge makes this process easy.

PHOTO F: Bevel-cut the edges of the roof sections and peak with a jig saw guided against a straightedge. Clamp the workpiece and straightedge to your worksurface to hold it steady while you cut.

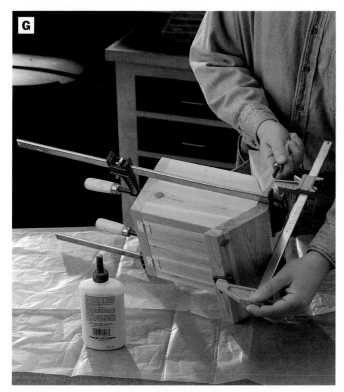

PHOTO G: Glue and clamp the roof parts together on the house assembly, then attach the roof with galvanized finish nails.

PHOTO H: Twist threaded eye hooks into pilot holes in the roof peak to prepare for hanging the project. Use a screwdriver to make turning the hooks easier.

⑮ Install the roof: Spread glue liberally on the mating edges of the roof parts as well as the top edges of the house front and back. Clamp the roof on the house so the roof overhangs the house evenly front to back (**See Photo G**). Drive 2-in. finish nails down through the roof parts into the house front and back to further secure the parts.

FINISHING TOUCHES

⑯ If you plan to hang the birdhouse, thread a pair of eye hooks into pilot holes in the roof peak, about 1½ in. in from the ends (**See Photo H**).

⑰ Form a "turnbuckle style" door latch by screwing a threaded "L" hook into an edge of the birdhouse back next to the door. Position the "L" hook so it holds the door closed when swiveled over the door.

⑱ Apply a protective topcoat of clear deck sealer, if you wish, to preserve the cedar's natural wood color.

HANGING INSTRUCTIONS

⑲ Hang the birdhouse from a sturdy tree limb, eave or other support at least 6 ft. from the ground. The house should be sheltered from prevailing winds.

Mounting option

If you'd rather mount this birdhouse to a post than hang it, drill pilot holes down through the bottom panel, and drive galvanized nails or a few screws into the post from inside the house. Another option is to attach the birdhouse to a post with small galvanized or brass angle brackets.

Simple Serving Tray

Don't get caught fumbling handfuls of cumbersome dishes and beverage containers ever again. Two hands will always be enough after this piece takes up residence in your home. Whether you're serving afternoon tea, popcorn and sodas or breakfast in bed, we've sized our oak tray to be as useful as it is handsome. Decorative corner guard hardware and matching brass handles add a touch of elegance to this hardworking accessory.

Simple Serving Tray: Step-by-step

PHOTO A: Glue the 36-in. lengths of quarter-round to the same-sized pieces of oak to prepare stock for the sides and ends. Arrange the molding so its curved profile will face down and in once the tray is assembled, with a flat surface facing up to support the tray bottom. Keep the bottom edges of both parts flush while you clamp the glue-up securely.

PREPARE THE SIDES

❶ Cut the stock for the tray sides into two 36-in. lengths. Do the same for the oak cleats.

❷ Attach the quarter-round cleats to the side stock pieces with glue to make two assemblies for miter-cutting. Be sure the molding profile faces the right way (See the technical drawing on page 110), and that the bottom edges of the parts are flush. Clamp the assemblies to your worksurface until the glue dries **(See Photo A).**

❸ Miter-cut the side and end pieces from the glued-up stock, using a back saw and miter box set to 45° **(See Photo B).** The two 36-in. lengths will yield one side piece and one end piece each.

Simple Serving Tray

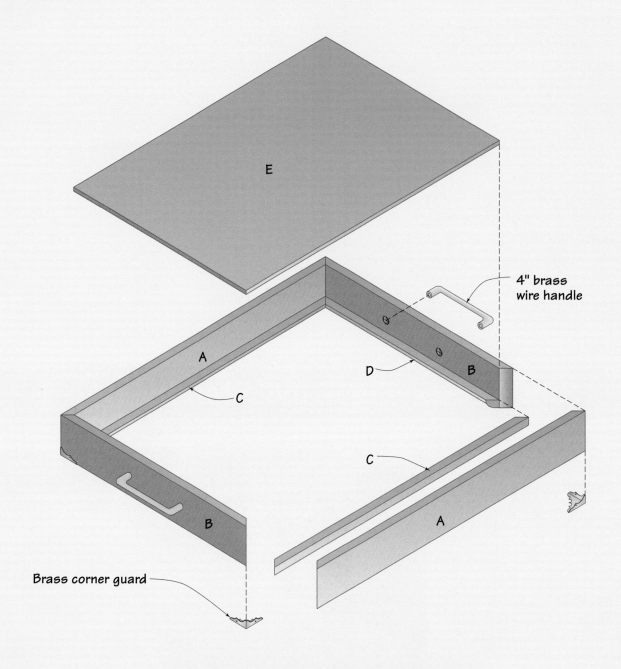

4" brass wire handle

E

A

C

D

B

B

C

A

Brass corner guard

Simple Serving Tray Cutting List

Part	No.	Size	Material
A. Sides	2	$\frac{1}{2} \times 2\frac{1}{2} \times 20$ in.	Red oak
B. Ends	2	$\frac{1}{2} \times 2\frac{1}{2} \times 14$ in.	"
C. Long cleats	2	$\frac{1}{2} \times \frac{1}{2} \times 19$ in.	Oak molding
D. Short cleats	2	$\frac{1}{2} \times \frac{1}{2} \times 13$ in.	"

ASSEMBLE THE TRAY

❹ Apply glue to the mating surfaces of the miter joints and assemble the tray. A frame clamp or strips of wide masking tape are good choices for holding the joints closed while the glue dries. Use a small square to check the corner joints to be sure they are square, and adjust if needed **(See Photo C).**

❺ Cut the plywood bottom to size.

❻ Once the frame assembly is dry, glue the bottom in place so it rests on the quarter-round cleats.

FINISHING TOUCHES

❼ After sanding the project, apply the stain of your choice, followed by two coats of varnish. We chose a golden oak stain to color our tray.

❽ Attach the corner guard hardware. Most of these are fastened with small brads made of the same material as the hardware, however some may be attached with screws. In either case, drill pilot holes before driving the fasteners to avoid splitting the oak at the edges.

❾ Locate the positions of the tray handles. Although the pulls are centered from side to side, they should be placed about 1½ in. up from the bottom for easier handling of the tray. Drill pilot holes and attach with the screws provided **(See Photo D).**

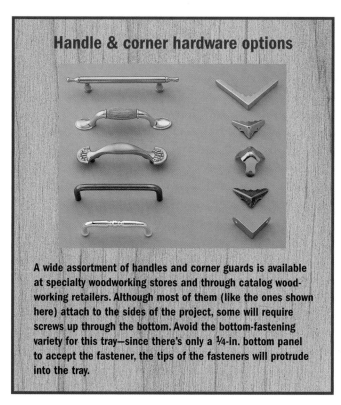

Handle & corner hardware options

A wide assortment of handles and corner guards is available at specialty woodworking stores and through catalog wood-working retailers. Although most of them (like the ones shown here) attach to the sides of the project, some will require screws up through the bottom. Avoid the bottom-fastening variety for this tray—since there's only a ¼-in. bottom panel to accept the fastener, the tips of the fasteners will protrude into the tray.

PHOTO B: Cut the sides and ends to length with 45° mitered ends, using a miter box. Push and pull the saw in long, fluid strokes to cut smoothly. Clamp the miter box securely in place while you cut.

PHOTO C: After you've applied glue to the mating ends of the mitered boards, assemble the sides. A frame clamp is a good choice for holding the mitered joints closed while the glue dries. Check for square corners before the glue sets.

PHOTO D: Attach the corner guard hardware first. Because you're working so close to the edge of the oak, drill pilot holes for the fasteners. Then locate the handle positions. These should be centered side to side, but slightly higher up from the bottom.

Funtime Toy Box

Playroom cleanup tasks will be much easier when kids can "feed" their toys to this whimsical whale toy box. You won't need a whale-sized budget to build this toy box either—all it takes is one sheet of plywood, some rope and a little paint. Rope handles make the lid easy to remove, and the absence of hinges means little fingers will be safe from pinching.

Vital statistics

TYPE: Toy box

OVERALL SIZE: 36L by 28H by 21½W

MATERIAL: Birch plywood

JOINERY: Butt joints reinforced with glue and screws

CONSTRUCTION DETAILS:
- The whale shapes are drawn to shape using a 1-in.-square grid pattern marked directly on the plywood
- Both whale sides are cut to shape with the gridded plywood pattern on top

FINISH: Primer and paint

BUILDING TIME: 4-6 hours

Shopping List

- ☐ ¾ in. × 4 × 8 ft. plywood
- ☐ Drywall screws (1¼-, 2-in.)
- ☐ ¾-in.-dia. × 2-ft. nylon rope
- ☐ Wood glue
- ☐ Finishing materials

Funtime Toy Box: Step-by-step

MAKE THE WHALE SIDES

To draw the whale profile, you could create a full-size paper template and trace the shape. It's more practical, however, to simply create a grid directly on the plywood, then use the grid drawing shown in the technical art, page 114, to mark points on your plywood grid for drawing the shape.

❶ Cut workpieces for the whale sides according to the *Cutting List,* page 114.

❷ Create a 1-in. square grid pattern on one of the two whale sides using a

PHOTO A: Create a full-size grid with 1-in. squares on one of the whale side blanks with a long T-square or straightedge and pencil.

Funtime Toy Box

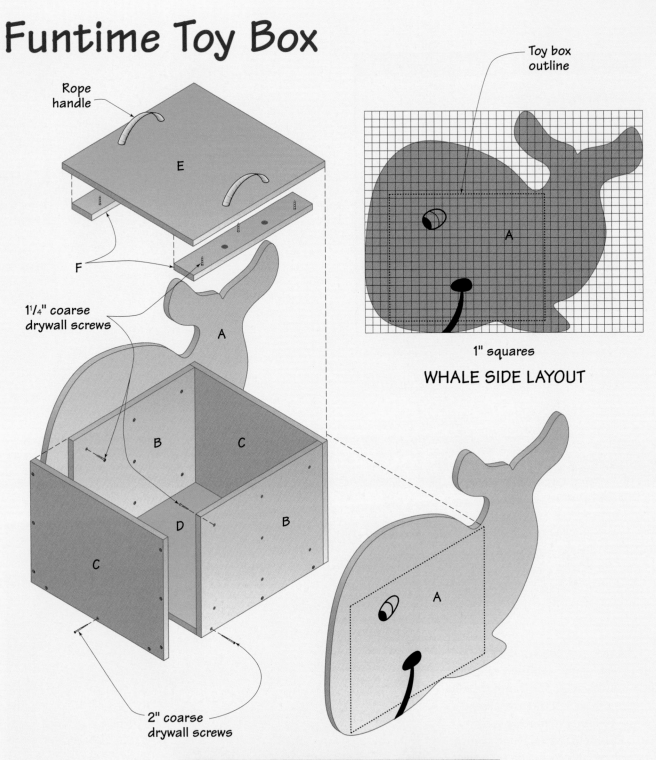

Rope handle

Toy box outline

E

F

1¼" coarse drywall screws

A

B C

D

B

C

2" coarse drywall screws

WHALE SIDE LAYOUT

1" squares

A

A

Funtime Toy Box Cutting List			
Part	No.	Size	Material
A. Whale sides	2	¾ × 28 × 36 in.	Plywood
B. Box sides	2	¾ × 18½ × 15¼ in.	"
C. Box front/back	2	¾ × 20 × 15¼ in.	"
D. Box bottom	1	¾ × 18½ × 18½ in.	"
E. Box lid	1	¾ × 19¾ × 20 in.	"
F. Lid battens	2	¾ × 3 × 18¼ in.	"

long T-square or straightedge and a pencil **(See Photo A).**

❸ Use a photocopier to enlarge the *Whale Side Layout* drawing on page 114 for easier reference when marking your grid.

❹ Mark points on the plywood grid squares that correspond to points on the paper reference to form a "dot-to-dot" pattern of the full-size whale profile. Connect the points with a solid pencil line to draw the whale shape. Follow the same procedure for drawing the whale eye **(See Photo B).**

❺ Cut the whale sides to shape: Stack the gridded whale side on top of the unmarked whale side. Elevate the workpieces off your worksurface with scrap 2 × 4s. Gang-cut both blanks to shape with a jig saw, keeping the workpieces aligned **(See Photo C).** Adjust the supports as needed to keep the cutting path clear.

ASSEMBLE THE BOX
❻ Cut the box sides, front, back and bottom to size.

❼ Build the box: Arrange the box sides, front and back around the box bottom so the front and back panels overlap the ends of the side panels. Apply glue to the mating surfaces of the box and clamp the box together. Reinforce the joints with countersunk 2-in. drywall screws **(See Photo D).**

BUILD THE LID
❽ Cut the plywood lid panel and two battens to size.

❾ Attach the battens to the lid. Lay out the positions of the battens on the lid so the battens are parallel to the 20-in.-long edges of the lid panel. Inset the battens

PHOTO B: Transfer layout points onto your plywood grid using an enlarged copy of the technical grid drawing as a reference. Connect the "dots" to draw the whale shape. Mark outlines for the eye and mouth as well.

PHOTO C: Stack the side with the grid drawing on top of the other side to gang-cut both whale side workpieces to shape. Raise the workpieces above the worksurface with scraps to provide clear space for the saw blade as you cut.

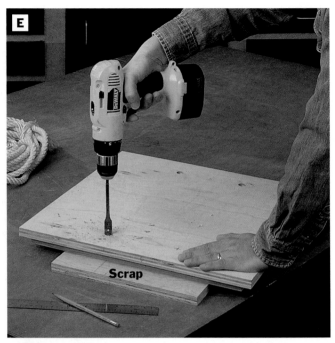

PHOTO D: Once you've glued and clamped the box sides, front and back around the box bottom, drill countersunk pilot holes and reinforce the joints with 2-in. drywall screws.

PHOTO E: Drill through the lid and battens for the rope handles. Use a spade bit of the same diameter as the rope you've chosen. Back up the hole you're drilling with scrap to reduce tearout.

PHOTO F: Paint the primary project color first on the whale sides, but leave the mouth and the black and white areas of the eye as primer only. Paint the mouth black. Then cut out regions of your paper eye template and use the template as a guide for finishing the eye details. A fine-tipped artist's brush is helpful for painting the small details.

⅞ in. from the ends of the lid and ¾ in. in from the edges. Spread glue on the battens and drive 1¼-in. drywall screws through the battens into the lid to secure the parts.

10 Drill pairs of holes in the lid for the rope handles: Locate each pair of holes 2 in. in from the long edges of the lid, spaced about 6 in. apart. Bore holes through the lid and battens (**See Photo E**).

PAINT THE TOY BOX

11 Fill the screwhead recesses and any plywood voids with wood putty. Sand the parts smooth.

12 Trace a paper template of the eye shape off of the gridded plywood whale side to use as a guide.

13 Prime and paint the lid, toy box and whale sides with the primary project color.

14 Paint the mouth and eye details. Cut out regions of the paper eye template as needed to help you paint the black and white eye areas (**See Photo F**).

FINISHING TOUCHES

15 Fasten the toy box to the whale sides: Center the toy box between the whale sides, using the *Whale Side Layout* drawing, page 114, as a guide. Support the toy box from beneath with scrap, and clamp the parts together. Drive 1¼-in. screws through the box and into the sides (**See Photo G**).

16 Make the handles: Cut two 10-in. lengths of nylon rope, tape the ends and thread the rope through the lid holes. Secure the handles with knots tied under the lid battens (**See Photo H**). Singe the ends of the rope with a flame to minimize fraying.

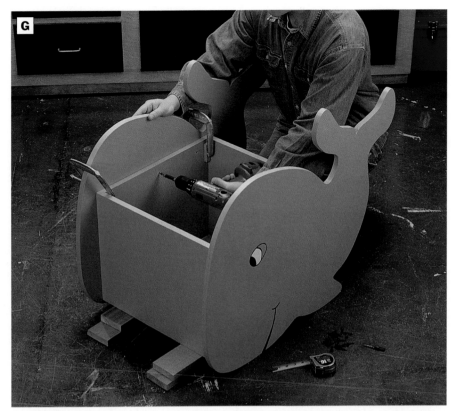

PHOTO G: Elevate the box on scrap blocks to attach the whale sides. Once you've positioned the parts properly, hold them in place with clamps and protective clamp pads. Attach the toy box to the whale sides with 1¼-in. drywall screws driven from inside the box.

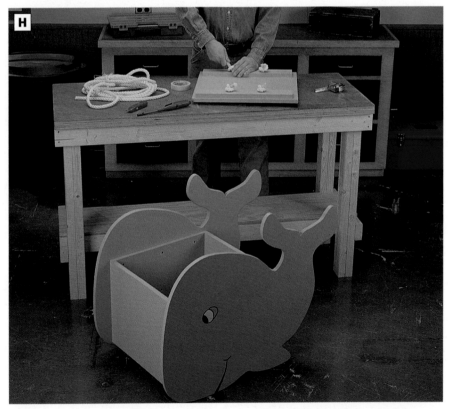

PHOTO H: Cut the rope handles to about 10 in. long, and wrap the ends with tape to make it easier to feed the ends through the lid holes. Insert the ropes in the lid and knot the ends.

Magazine Rack

Keep magazines and other periodicals neatly organized and within easy reach when you display them in this wall-mounted oak magazine rack. Two compartments provide ample storage space, yet the rack only projects 3½ in. at its widest point from a wall. For a decorative touch, we use pre-milled oak door stop to make the slats.

Magazine Rack: Step-by-step

CUT THE PARTS

1 Crosscut two 20-in. pieces of oak for the side pieces and one 19¼-in. strip for the divider.

2 Draw the shapes of the sides. Refer to the *Side Layout* drawing, page 120, to lay out the profiles of these parts. Use a compass to scribe 1-in.-radius curves on the top outside corners.

3 Cut the sides to shape with a jig saw, and smooth the cut edges with a file.

4 Lay out and cut the divider. The overall shape of the divider matches the sides, but the divider is ¾ in. shorter and has a notched cut-out at the top to wrap around the back rail. Use

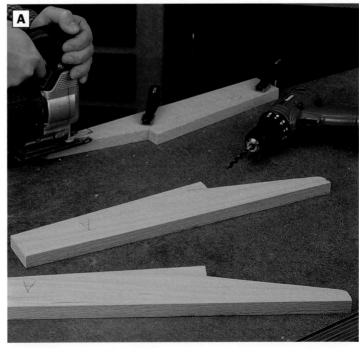

PHOTO A: Cut the sides and divider to shape with a jig saw. It's easiest to cut these parts if you clamp each workpiece to your worksurface. Drill clearance holes in the corners of the divider notch to provide clearance for turning the blade when making the bottom notch cut.

Magazine Rack

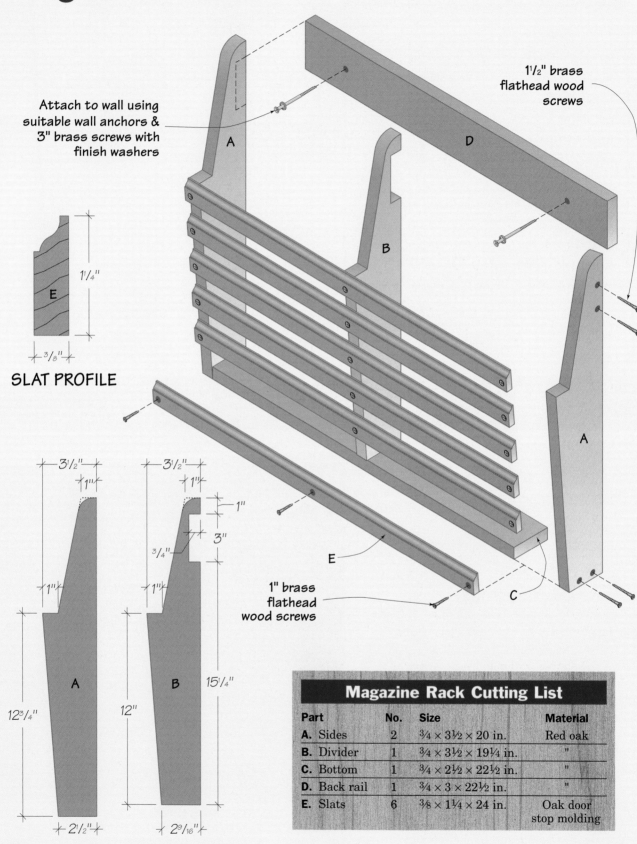

Attach to wall using suitable wall anchors & 3" brass screws with finish washers

1½" brass flathead wood screws

A

D

B

A

SLAT PROFILE

1¼"

³⁄₈"

E

1" brass flathead wood screws

E

C

SIDE LAYOUT

3½"

1"

1"

A

12³⁄₄"

2½"

DIVIDER LAYOUT

3½"

1"

1"

3"

¾"

1"

B

15¼"

12"

2⁹⁄₁₆"

Magazine Rack Cutting List

Part	No.	Size	Material
A. Sides	2	¾ × 3½ × 20 in.	Red oak
B. Divider	1	¾ × 3½ × 19¼ in.	"
C. Bottom	1	¾ × 2½ × 22½ in.	"
D. Back rail	1	¾ × 3 × 22½ in.	"
E. Slats	6	³⁄₈ × 1¼ × 24 in.	Oak door stop molding

one of the side pieces to trace the divider shape. See the *Divider Layout* drawing, page 120, to mark the ¾-in.-deep, 3-in.-long cutout. Cut out the divider with a jig saw **(See Photo A).**

5 Rip and crosscut the bottom and back rail to size. Crosscut the six slats to length.

6 Sand all the parts smooth.

ASSEMBLE THE MAGAZINE RACK

7 Test the fit of the back rail in the divider notch, then fasten the back rail to the divider with glue and a couple of countersunk 1-in. screws, driven through the back rail into the divider notch.

8 Install the sides and bottom on the back rail and divider: The sides overlap the ends of the back rail, and the top edge of the back rail is inset 1 in. down from the top ends of the sides. The bottom fits between the sides, flush with their bottom ends and against the bottom end of the divider. Spread glue on the mating surfaces of these joints, clamp the parts in place and attach them with pairs of countersunk 1½-in. flathead wood screws **(See Photo B).**

9 Apply finish to all surfaces of the magazine rack assembly and slats **(See Photo C).**

10 Install the slats: Arrange the slats on the rack so their profiled edges face up. The top slat should be even with the 1-in. notches on the sides and divider. The bottom slat is flush with the bottom of the project. Space the remaining four slats evenly (1¹⁄₁₆-in. spaces between slats). Attach the slats to the sides and divider with countersunk 1-in. brass screws, one screw per joint **(See Photo D).**

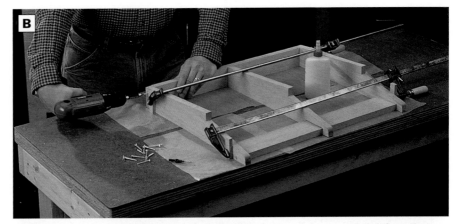

PHOTO B: Glue and clamp the sides to the ends of the bottom and upper rail. Reinforce these joints with countersunk 1½-in. brass wood screws.

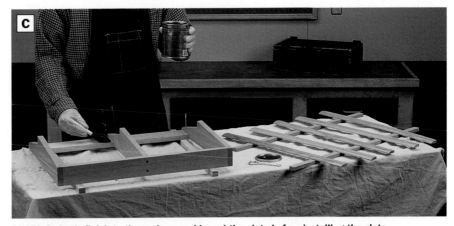

PHOTO C: Apply finish to the rack assembly and the slats before installing the slats. Prefinishing the parts while they're fully accessible is easier and faster than waiting until after the slats are installed.

PHOTO D: Attach the slats to the front edges of the sides and divider with countersunk 1-in. brass wood screws. Lay out the slats so they're spaced evenly apart on the rack.

Kid's Wall Clock

Kids will find it tougher to lose track of time when it's marked on the belly of their favorite animal or storybook character. We're providing three animal patterns here, but the simple plywood clock back design could be adapted to any shape you like.

Vital statistics

TYPE: Wall clock

OVERALL SIZE: Varies with clock shape

MATERIAL: Plywood

JOINERY: None

CONSTRUCTION DETAILS:
- Clock shapes made by tracing around a full-size template
- Hole for clock insert cut with a hole saw and drill

FINISH: Primer and paint

BUILDING TIME: 1-2 hours

Shopping List

- ☐ (1) ¾ in. × 2 × 4 ft. birch plywood
- ☐ (1) ¼ in. × 2 × 4 ft. hardboard
- ☐ Spray mount adhesive
- ☐ (1) 4⅜-in.-dia. battery-powered quartz clock insert
- ☐ Two-part epoxy (optional)
- ☐ Picture-hanging hardware
- ☐ Finishing materials

Kid's Wall Clock: Step-by-step

MAKE A CLOCK BACK TEMPLATE

❶ The easiest way to draw the shape of the clock back onto your plywood is to begin with a full-size paper pattern and trace the shape. You can make a more durable template by gluing your paper pattern to a piece of hardboard, as we show here.

❷ Choose and enlarge a grid drawing shown in the technical art, page 124, on a photocopier to produce a full-size paper pattern.

❸ Mount the paper pattern to a

PHOTO A: Enlarge the grid drawing about 400% of its original size to create a full-size paper template for tracing the shape of the clock back. We adhered the paper pattern onto a piece of hardboard to make the template more rigid, then cut out the template shape.

Kid's Wall Clock

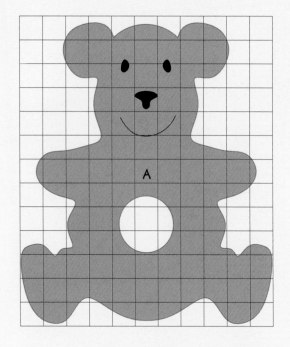

TEDDY BEAR PATTERN

All grid squares are 1". Enlarge to 400% to create a full-size pattern.

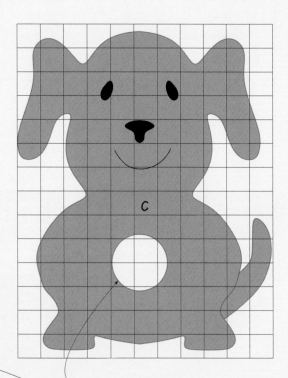

DOG PATTERN

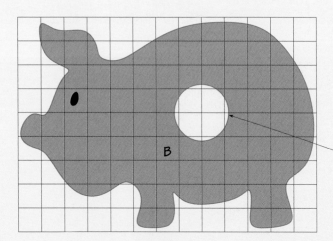

PIG PATTERN

Size hole for clock insert according to manufacturer's specifications.

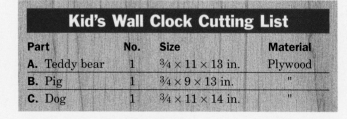

Kid's Wall Clock Cutting List			
Part	No.	Size	Material
A. Teddy bear	1	¾ × 11 × 13 in.	Plywood
B. Pig	1	¾ × 9 × 13 in.	"
C. Dog	1	¾ × 11 × 14 in.	"

PHOTO B: Trace the template shape onto a piece of plywood, then cut out the clock back with a jig saw.

PHOTO C: Bore a clock insert hole with a hole saw chucked in a drill. Support the cut from beneath with a backer board.

piece of hardboard. We used spray mount adhesive, available at craft stores (**See Photo A**). You could also apply the pattern to the hardboard with a thin coat of white glue or double-sided tape.

4 Cut the hardboard template to shape with a jig saw, and smooth the cut edges with sandpaper.

MAKE THE CLOCK BACK

5 Cut a piece of plywood to size for the clock back, according to the *Cutting List,* page 124.

6 Trace the clock back shape onto the plywood using your full-size template (**See Photo B**).

7 Cut out the clock back shape with a jig saw and fine-toothed blade.

8 Fill any voids in the edges of the plywood clock back with wood putty, and sand the workpiece smooth when the putty dries.

9 Prime and paint the clock back. Add details like eyes, nose and mouth with an artist's brush.

INSTALL THE CLOCK INSERT

10 Cut out the clock insert hole. An easy way to do this is to first set the template in place over the clock back and drill a small pilot hole through the center of the clock pattern. Use this as a centerpoint on the clock back for cutting the clock insert hole with a hole saw (**See Photo C**).

11 Install the clock insert in the clock back. Glue the insert to the clock back permanently, if you wish, with two-part epoxy.

FINISHING TOUCHES

12 Attach sturdy picture-hanging hardware to the clock back so the clock hangs evenly.

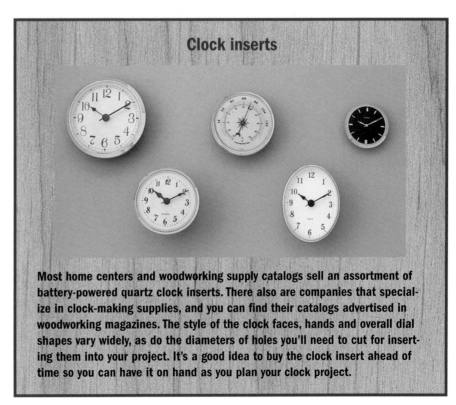

Clock inserts

Most home centers and woodworking supply catalogs sell an assortment of battery-powered quartz clock inserts. There also are companies that specialize in clock-making supplies, and you can find their catalogs advertised in woodworking magazines. The style of the clock faces, hands and overall dial shapes vary widely, as do the diameters of holes you'll need to cut for inserting them into your project. It's a good idea to buy the clock insert ahead of time so you can have it on hand as you plan your clock project.

Recipe Holder

Build this handy kitchen organizer for the cook in your household, and your efforts may truly earn sweet rewards. A recipe card drawer with divider stores several generations' worth of family favorites. The "easel-style" cookbook rest holds a cookbook open and in full view and keeps it from gobbling up precious countertop workspace.

Shopping List

- ☐ (1) ½ in. × 2 × 4 ft. birch plywood
- ☐ (1) Threaded drawer pull
- ☐ (4) Nail-on nylon drawer glides
- ☐ 1¼-in. finish nails
- ☐ Wood glue
- ☐ Finishing materials

Recipe Holder: Step-by-step

BUILD THE COOKBOOK REST

❶ Lay out and cut the book rest, shelf and shelf lip according to the dimensions given in the *Cutting List,* page 128.

❷ Fasten the shelf on edge to the book rest so it's flush with the bottom edge of the front. Secure these parts with glue and 1¼-in. finish nails.

❸ Attach the shelf lip to the front edge of the shelf so the bottom edge of the lip is flush with the bottom face of the shelf. Glue and nail the parts together. Recess the nailheads with a nailset **(See Photo A).**

PHOTO A: Assemble the book rest, shelf and shelf lip with glue and 1¼-in. finish nails. Drill pilot holes first for the nails.

Recipe Holder

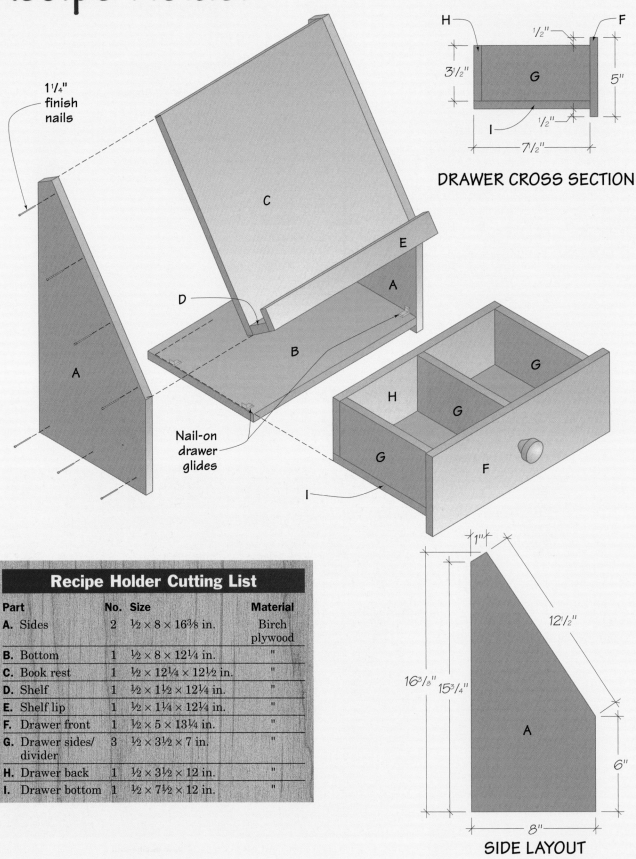

1¼" finish nails

H

½"

F

3½"

G

5"

I

½"

7½"

DRAWER CROSS SECTION

C

E

A

D

B

G

H

G

G

Nail-on drawer glides

G

F

I

Recipe Holder Cutting List

Part	No.	Size	Material
A. Sides	2	½ × 8 × 16⅜ in.	Birch plywood
B. Bottom	1	½ × 8 × 12¼ in.	"
C. Book rest	1	½ × 12¼ × 12½ in.	"
D. Shelf	1	½ × 1½ × 12¼ in.	"
E. Shelf lip	1	½ × 1¼ × 12¼ in.	"
F. Drawer front	1	½ × 5 × 13¼ in.	"
G. Drawer sides/ divider	3	½ × 3½ × 7 in.	"
H. Drawer back	1	½ × 3½ × 12 in.	"
I. Drawer bottom	1	½ × 7½ × 12 in.	"

1"

12½"

16⅜"

15¾"

A

6"

8"

SIDE LAYOUT

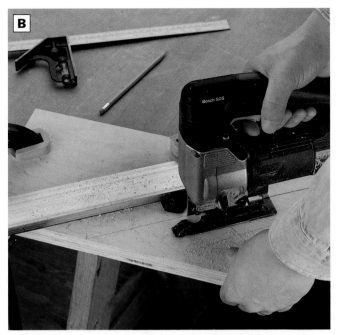

PHOTO B: Lay out and cut the side panels to shape with a jig saw guided by a clamped straightedge.

PHOTO C: Glue and nail the sides to the bottom and cookbook rest to form the recipe box. Arrange and clamp the parts so you can nail through one side, then reclamp and fasten the other side.

ASSEMBLE THE RECIPE HOLDER

④ Make the sides: Rip and crosscut two 8-in.-wide, 16⅜-in.-long pieces of plywood for the side workpieces. Follow the *Side Layout* drawing, page 128, to lay out the angled shapes of the sides. Cut the sides to shape with a jig saw (**See Photo B**).

⑤ Cut the plywood bottom panel to size.

⑥ Build the recipe box: Draw reference lines across the inside faces of the box sides ½ in. up from the bottom to mark the location of the box bottom. Spread glue on the edges of the front panel of the cookbook rest, as well as on the ends of the bottom panel. Clamp the cookbook rest and the bottom panel between the sides, configuring the parts so the project is lying on its side. Be sure the bottom panel lines up with the reference lines and the cookbook rest is flush with the angled profiles on the side panels. Drill pilot holes and drive 1¼-in. finish nails through the side panel into both the bottom and cookbook rest. Set the nailheads. Reclamp the project so the other side panel is on top, and nail these joints in the same fashion (**See Photo C**).

BUILD THE DRAWER

⑦ Rip and crosscut all of the drawer parts to size.

⑧ Fasten the drawer bottom to the back in the orientation shown in the *Drawer Cross Section* drawing,

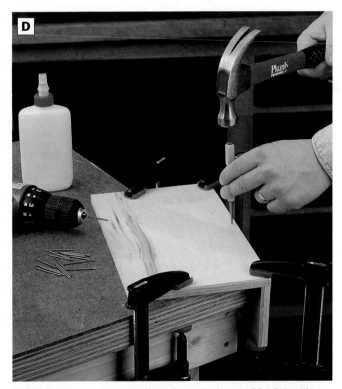

PHOTO D: Glue, clamp and nail the drawer bottom and back together. Drive the nails through pilot holes, and recess the nailheads with a nailset.

page 128. Spread glue along one long edge of the drawer bottom before clamping the two parts together, then drill pilot holes through the bottom and into the back. Attach the parts with 1¼-in. finish nails (**See Photo D**).

PHOTO E: Fasten the drawer sides and divider to the bottom and back with the drawer arranged upside down on your bench. Glue, clamp and nail these joints.

PHOTO F: Install the drawer front on the drawer carcase with glue and finish nails. Note that the front overhangs the drawer carcase ⅝ in. on the sides and ½ in. on the top and bottom.

9 Add the drawer sides and divider: Mark the centerline of the drawer divider across the bottom face of the drawer bottom. Spread glue along one short end and one long edge of the drawer sides and divider. Set the drawer parts together on your bench with the drawer bottom facing up. Drive finish nails through pilot holes in the drawer bottom and back and into the sides and divider to fasten the parts (**See Photo E**).

10 Install the drawer front on the drawer carcase: Set the drawer front on the drawer carcase so it overhangs each drawer side by ⅝ in., but only ½ in. on the top and bottom. Mark centerlines on the drawer front for the sides, divider and bottom. Spread glue on the front edges of the drawer carcase, clamp the drawer front in place and attach it with finish nails. Set the nailheads (**See Photo F**).

FINISHING TOUCHES

11 Fill nailhead recesses and any other voids in the plywood with wood putty. Sand the project thoroughly.

12 Apply primer and two coats of paint.

13 Install a drawer pull at the center of the drawer front (**See Photo G**).

14 Nail four drawer glides to the recipe box bottom so they're flush with the side panels. Locate a pair of glides about 1½ in. from the front of the drawer opening and another pair 4 in. in from the back (**See Photo H**).

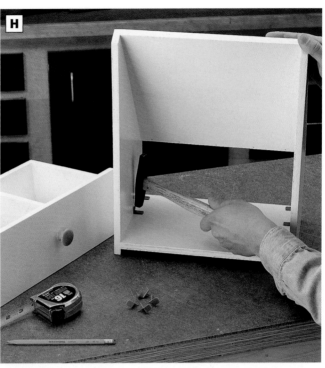

PHOTO G: Drill a pilot hole at the center of the drawer front for a threaded drawer pull. Install the pull.

PHOTO H: Tack four nail-on nylon drawer glides to the recipe box bottom inside the drawer opening. The glides should be flush against the project sides.

Stencils & stamps

Decorate this recipe holder with kitchen themes using stencils or stamps available at most craft and discount stores. To transfer an image, simply hold or tape the stencil in place, apply paint in the cutout areas and lift off the stencil for reuse. If you use plastic sheet stencils, it's a good idea to apply them with gel-style stencil paint or spray paint instead of thinner, brush-on paint. Thin paints tend to bleed beneath the stenciled areas, ruining the desired shape. Another detailing option is to buy foam-rubber stamps with raised shapes that you cover with paint and stamp on the project.

Window Box

Brighten your view and add a touch more "curb appeal" to your home by outfitting your windows with these window boxes. We've kept the design simple so the style conforms to most any home style. Simplicity also means you can build several window boxes in one shop session. You'll find hanging these boxes is a snap, too, thanks to a pair of interlocking beveled cleats that hide behind the project when it's installed.

Vital statistics

TYPE: Window box

OVERALL SIZE: 36½L by 8H by 11¾D

MATERIAL: Cedar

JOINERY: Butt joints reinforced with glue and screws or galvanized finish nails

CONSTRUCTION DETAILS:
- Decorative curved edges on front panel are cut with a jig saw
- Project installs with a pair of bevel-edged hanging cleats
- Exterior fasteners used throughout to resist corrosion
- Project designed to fit a standard planter insert measuring 30L by 6H by 8D

FINISH: Stain and/or wood preservative; could also be left unfinished

BUILDING TIME: 3-4 hours

Shopping List

- ☐ (1) 1 × 8 in. × 8 ft. cedar*
- ☐ (1) 1 × 6 in. × 4 ft. cedar*
- ☐ (2) 1 × 2 in. × 10 ft. cedar*
- ☐ 2-in. galvanized finish nails
- ☐ 1¼-in. deck screws
- ☐ Moisture-resistant wood glue
- ☐ Finishing materials (optional)

*We used cedar here, but other suitable woods for outdoor projects can be found on page 137.

Window Box: Step-by-step

BUILD THE BOX

❶ Crosscut the cedar boards for the front, back and two end pieces according to the dimensions given in the *Cutting List,* page 134.

❷ Refer to the *Front Layout* drawing, page 134, to draw the curved profiles on both ends of the front panel. Clamp the front panel to a worksurface and cut the curved profiles with a jig saw (**See Photo A**). Smooth the curves with sandpaper.

PHOTO A: Cut the curved profiles on the ends of the front panel with a jig saw.

Window Box

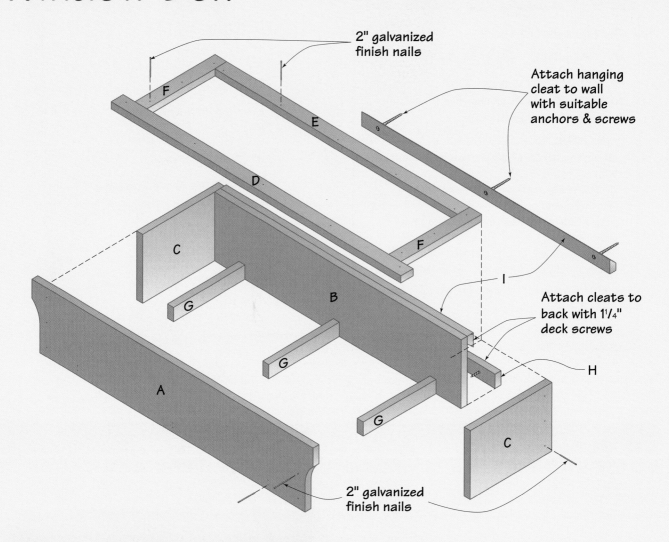

2" galvanized finish nails

Attach hanging cleat to wall with suitable anchors & screws

F

E

D

C

B

A

G

G

G

I

Attach cleats to back with 1¼" deck screws

H

C

2" galvanized finish nails

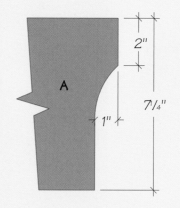

Window Box Cutting List

Part	No.	Size	Material
A. Front	1	⅞ × 7¼ × 35½ in.	Cedar
B. Back	1	⅞ × 7¼ × 31 in.	"
C. Sides	2	⅞ × 7¼ × 10¼ in.	"
D. Front trim	1	⅞ × 1½ × 36½ in.	"
E. Back trim	1	⅞ × 1½ × 30½ in.	"
F. Side trim	2	⅞ × 1½ × 10 in.	"
G. Bottom supports	3	⅞ × 1½ × 9 in.	"
H. Blocking	1	⅞ × 1½ × 31 in.	"
I. Hanging cleats	2	⅞ × 1½ × 31 in.	"

A

2"

7¼"

1"

FRONT LAYOUT

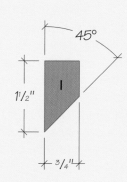

45°

I

1½"

¾"

HANGING CLEAT

3 Attach the sides to the front panel: Draw reference lines across the inside back face of the front panel, 1½ in. in from either end. Spread glue on one end of each side piece and set the sides in place on the front panel so the outside faces of the sides align with the reference lines on the front panel. Attach the parts with 2-in. galvanized finish nails driven through the front and into the sides.

4 Install the back: Set the back in place between the sides, spaced 9 in. from the back face of the front panel. Mark this location and remove the back. Spread glue on the ends of the back, slip it into place between the sides and clamp the parts. Fasten the sides to the back with galvanized finish nails. Recess the nailheads with a nailset (**See Photo B**).

INSTALL THE BOTTOM SUPPORTS

5 Crosscut three 9-in. bottom supports from cedar 1 × 2. Mark locations for the bottom supports inside the box on the front and back panels. Position one support so it will be centered on the length of the box. Locate the other two supports 2 in. in from the sides.

6 Test-fit the bottom supports in the window box, arranging the supports so the narrow edges are flush with the bottom edges of the box front and back. Then spread glue on the ends of the supports and clamp them in place inside the box. Fasten the supports with galvanized finish nails driven through pilot holes in the box front and back (**See Photo C**).

PHOTO B: Glue and clamp the box back in place between the sides, and fasten the parts with galvanized finish nails. Recess the nailheads with a nailset.

PHOTO C: Glue and nail the three bottom supports in the box so the narrow edges are flush with the bottom edges of the box. Set the nailheads below the surface.

ADD THE TRIM

7 Crosscut the trim front, back and two end pieces to length from cedar 1 × 2. Position the front trim piece on the top edge of the box front so it overhangs the ends and face of the box front by ½ in. Glue and nail the front trim piece.

8 Install the trim ends on the box ends so they butt against the back of the front trim piece and overhang the outside face of the box ends by ½ in. Glue and nail the trim ends in place.

9 Glue and nail the back trim piece over the box back and between the trim ends. Align this trim piece so its outside edge is flush with the back ends of the trim end pieces.

10 Recess all of the nails holding the trim in place with a nailset (**See Photo D**).

PHOTO D: Install the four trim pieces around the top edges of the window box with moisture-resistant wood glue and nails. The front and end trim pieces should overhang the box by ½ in.

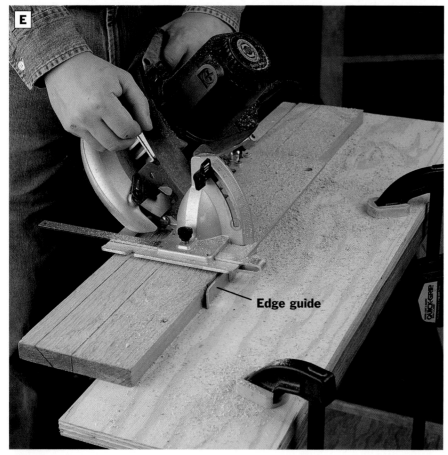

Edge guide

PHOTO E: Lay out the hanging cleats so you can cut the beveled edges in one pass. We cut the strips from a cedar 1 × 6 to provide adequate support for the saw base. We also screwed the cedar board near its edge to a strip of plywood to provide clearance below for the saw blade. An edge guide installed on the saw base makes these bevel-rip cuts easier to perform accurately.

INSTALL THE HANGING CLEATS & BLOCKING

The window box is designed with a pair of bevel-edged hanging cleats to make mounting the box easy. One cleat fastens to the window box with the bevel edge facing down and toward the window box. The other cleat attaches to a windowsill or house siding with the bevel edge facing up and toward the house. In these alternating positions, the cleat bevels interlock when the window box is hung in place.

⓫ Lay out and cut the hanging cleats: You can cut bevels for both cleats in one saw pass if you lay out the cleats in the interlocked position along the edge of a 31-in. length of cedar 1 × 6. Cutting the cleats from a wide board also provides more support for your saw base. Set your circular saw or jig saw to cut a 45° bevel, and rip the first cleat from the board, cutting along the bevel-edge layout line **(See Photo E).** Reset the saw to 90° and rip-cut the second cleat from the board.

⓬ Install one hanging cleat on the window box: Mount the cleat beneath the back trim overhang so the beveled edge faces down and inward. Fasten the parts with 1¼-in. deck screws.

⓭ Crosscut the blocking piece to length from cedar 1 × 2. Attach the blocking with screws so it is flush with the bottom back edge of the window box **(See Photo F).**

FINISH & MOUNT THE WINDOW BOX

⓮ Apply several coats of stain or clear outdoor wood preservative to the window box and remaining hanging cleat. You also can leave the wood bare, if you prefer, so it "weathers" naturally to a silvery gray color.

15 Choose a location for the window box that will be easy to access for planting and seasonal clean-out. Mount the remaining hanging cleat to the house so the beveled edge faces up and toward the house. When positioning the cleat on the house, keep in mind that the window box top edge will be 1½ in. higher than the top edge of the cleat. Fasten the cleat with long deck screws to a windowsill or directly to the house siding. Try to drive the screws so they'll hit wall framing members behind the house siding.

16 Hang the window box by interlocking the hanging cleats. If you want to mount the box permanently, drive additional screws through the box back and blocking into the house siding.

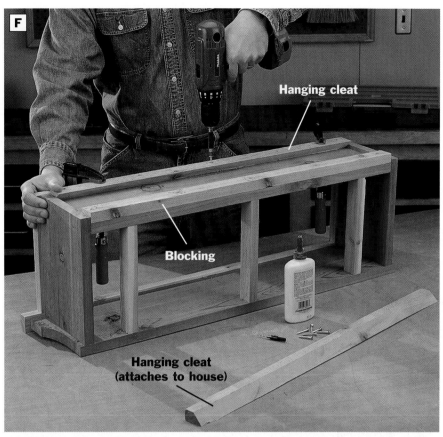

PHOTO F: Attach one hanging cleat and the blocking strip to the back of the window box with 1¼-in. deck screws and moisture-resistant wood glue. The other hanging cleat attaches to the house with deck screws.

Choosing woods for outdoor projects

Outdoor wood furniture can survive for many years in the elements, but you need to choose wood carefully. A number of wood species contain natural oils that make them more resistant to rotting, insect infestation and degradation from ultraviolet sunlight than other woods. We use Western red cedar for several projects in this book, but other excellent wood choices for outdoor projects include redwood, teak, cypress, white oak and Honduras mahogany. Some of these varieties are harder to find in many areas of the United States and can be quite expensive.

Treated lumber and exterior-grade plywood are also good options for outdoor projects, but you'll probably want to reserve these wood products for projects you plan to paint. Treated lumber is pressure-infused with chemicals that make it insect- and moisture-resistant. Exterior-grade plywood is made with waterproof glue, so it resists delaminating when it comes into contact with moisture.

Other less weather-durable woods, like red oak and pine, can be used for outdoor projects as well, but these woods must be topcoated thoroughly with primer and paint or

Naturally weather-resistant woods include, from left to right, redwood, cedar, white oak and teak.

other UV-protective sealers. It's a good idea to keep projects made from these woods in an area sheltered from moisture or direct ground contact and store them inside during seasons when they aren't in use.

Full-shelter Doghouse

Keep a canine friend warm and dry in this sturdy doghouse. Our design features a dividing wall that provides complete shelter from wind and rain, and the shingled roof is removable for easier cleaning. In colder climates, you can even install sheet foam insulation beneath the floor for added warmth.

Vital statistics

TYPE: Doghouse

OVERALL SIZE: 48L by 40W by 44H

MATERIAL: Exterior plywood, roofing materials

JOINERY: Butt joints reinforced with glue and screws

CONSTRUCTION DETAILS:
- Gussets beneath the roof panels strengthen the roof so it can be lifted off
- Roof sealed against weather with 15-pound building paper and asphalt shingles

FINISH: Exterior primer and paint

BUILDING TIME: 8-10 hours

Shopping List

- ☐ (3) ¾ in. × 4 ft. × 8 ft. exterior plywood
- ☐ (1) ¾ in. × 4 ft. × 4 ft. exterior plywood
- ☐ 2-in. deck screws
- ☐ Moisture-resistant wood glue
- ☐ 15-pound building paper
- ☐ Asphalt shingles
- ☐ Galvanized staples
- ☐ Roofing nails
- ☐ Finishing materials

Full-shelter Doghouse: Step-by-step

The proportions of this doghouse project are intended for housing medium to large dog breeds. Contact a dog breeder or your local branch of the Humane Society for information on suitable doghouse sizes for smaller dogs.

MAKE THE DOGHOUSE PARTS

❶ Cut two 40 × 40-in. pieces of plywood for the front and back panels. Follow the *Front Layout* drawing, page 140, to draw the angled roof profiles as well as the arch-top door opening. Cut the roof angles.

PHOTO A: Draw the arch-top door opening on the doghouse front panel, and cut out the opening with a jig saw. Drill a starter hole in the cutout area first, so you can insert the saw blade to begin the cut.

Full-shelter Doghouse

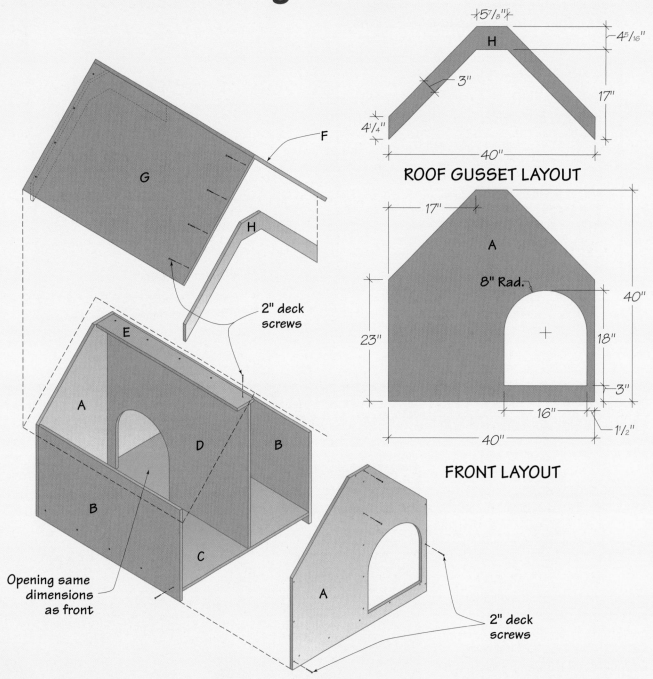

ROOF GUSSET LAYOUT

5⁷/₈"
H
4⁵/₁₆"
3"
17"
4¹/₄"
40"

FRONT LAYOUT

17"
A
8" Rad.
40"
23"
18"
3"
16"
40"
1¹/₂"

F
G
H
2" deck screws

E
A
D
B
B
C

Opening same dimensions as front

A
2" deck screws

Full-shelter Doghouse Cutting List

Part	No.	Size	Material	Part	No.	Size	Material
A. Front/back	2	¾ × 40 × 40 in.	Exterior plywood	**E.** Interior brace	1	¾ × 5 × 42½ in.	Exterior plywood
B. Sides	2	¾ × 42½ × 23 in.	"	**F.** Roof (long)	1	¾ × 48 × 31 in.	"
C. Bottom	1	¾ × 38½ × 42½ in.	"	**G.** Roof (short)	1	¾ × 48 × 30¼ in.	"
D. Interior divider	1	¾ × 36¼ × 42½ in.	"	**H.** Roof gussets	2	¾ × 21⁵/₁₆ × 40 in.	"

❷ Cut the door opening in the front with a jig saw. Start the cut by drilling a pilot hole in one corner of the door layout area, large enough to insert the saw blade for starting the cut **(See Photo A).**

❸ Rip and crosscut the two side panels, bottom and the interior brace to size.

❹ Make the interior divider: Cut a plywood work-piece to size, following the *Cutting List* dimensions on page 140. Lay the doghouse front panel on the divider workpiece and use the front door opening as a template for drawing a door on the divider. Locate the door so it's flush with the bottom edge of the divider and 2 in. in from the end. Trace the door on the divider and cut the opening.

ASSEMBLE THE DOGHOUSE

❺ Fasten the front and back panels to the sides. Arrange the parts so the front and back overlap the ends of the side panels. Spread moisture-resistant wood glue on the ends of the sides and clamp the four parts together. TIP: *If you don't have clamps long enough to hold these parts together, stretch duct tape over the joints instead.* Drill countersunk pilot holes through the front and back and into the ends of the sides. Attach the parts with 2-in. deck screws.

❻ Install the bottom: Draw a reference line 3 in. up from the bottom edges of the doghouse assembly all the way around the inside of the structure. This line represents the top face of the doghouse bottom panel; it should align with the flat bottom edge of the front door. Slip the bottom panel into position and attach it with countersunk deck screws driven through the front, back and sides **(See Photo B).**

❼ Attach the interior divider: Draw vertical reference lines on the front and back panels for locating the divider inside the doghouse. Measure and mark these lines 20 in. in from the left side of the doghouse (when viewed from the front). Slide the interior divider into position so the divider door is positioned near the back of the doghouse. Secure the divider by driving 2-in. countersunk deck screws through the front, back and bottom panels.

❽ Install the interior brace: Set the interior brace so it caps the top edge of the divider and is centered on the short, flat top edges of the front and back panels. Drive 2-in. deck screws down through the brace into the divider as well as through the front and back

PHOTO B: Fasten the bottom panel in place between the front, back and side pieces with countersunk deck screws. Position the bottom 3 in. up from the bottom edges of the parts and so the top face is flush with the bottom of the door opening.

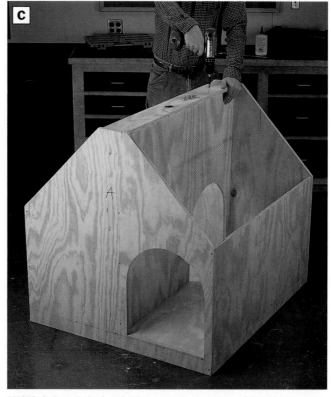

PHOTO C: Install the interior brace on the top edge of the divider and so it is centered on the short, flat top edges of the doghouse front and back. Fasten the parts with screws.

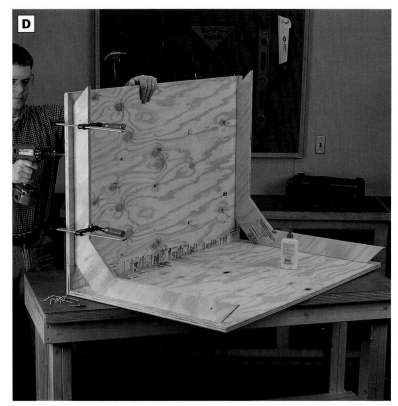

PHOTO D: Assemble the roof panels and gussets to form the roof structure. Allow for a 1-in. overhang between the ends of the roof and the gussets. Fasten the parts with glue and countersunk deck screws.

PHOTO E: Prime and paint the doghouse surfaces, inside and out. Seal the bottom edges with primer and paint, to keep the plywood from wicking up ground moisture.

panels to fasten the brace in place (**See Photo C**).

BUILD THE ROOF STRUCTURE

The doghouse roof is designed to be a removable unit, to make cleaning out the interior of the house easier. A pair of gussets beneath the roof panels stiffen the structure and hold the roof panels at 90° to one another.

9 Rip and crosscut the two roof sections. Follow the *Cutting List* dimensions carefully—the roof panels differ in width so one panel can overlap the other at the roof peak, once installed.

10 Make the roof gussets: To lay out the gusset shape, mark a 20 × 40-in. rectangle on a plywood sheet, and follow the *Roof Gusset Layout* drawing, page 140, to draw the shape within this rectangle. Cut out the gusset with a jig saw or circular saw. Use the first gusset as a template for drawing the second gusset shape, then cut out the second gusset.

11 Assemble the roof panels: Spread glue along one long edge of the narrower roof panel, and set the wider roof panel against the first so it overlaps the glued edge and the parts meet at 90°. Drive countersunk 2-in. deck screws through the joint to fasten the roof panels together.

12 Install the gussets: Mark the inside faces of the roof panels with layout lines for gussets. The roof should overhang each gusset by 1 in. Spread moisture-resistant glue along the top long edges of the gussets, and clamp each gusset in place on the roof panels. Drive countersunk 2-in. deck screws through the roof panels and into the gussets (**See Photo D**).

APPLY FINISH

13 Sand the doghouse inside and out, as well as ease any sharp cut edges, especially around the doors.

14 Prepare the plywood for paint with a

PHOTO F: Staple a layer of building paper over the roof panels, then shingle the roof, starting from the bottom and working up to the peak.

PHOTO G: We stenciled the name of our project's future resident on the doghouse front.

coat of exterior primer. Prime all surfaces, including the bottom edges of the doghouse that will come in contact with the ground. Topcoat with exterior paint **(See Photo E).**

SHINGLE THE ROOF

15 Cut and staple 15-pound building paper over the outer faces of the roof panels. Be sure the seams overlap at least 6 in. in the peak area to seal out leaks.

16 Install asphalt shingles over the building paper with roofing nails, just as you would shingle any roof. Start at the bottom and work your way up the roof, overlapping each course of shingles and staggering the shingle slots **(See Photo F).** Protect the roof peak with a row of overlapped shingle "ridge caps" nailed in place.

FINISHING TOUCHES

17 Stencil the dog's name on the project if you like, to add a personal touch **(See Photo G).**

18 In cold climates, install rigid foam insulation beneath the bottom panel (See *Adding insulation,* right).

Adding insulation

This doghouse project was designed to accept a sheet of 1-in.-thick rigid foam insulation below the bottom panel. Rigid foam is a good choice because it is relatively inexpensive and unaffected by ground moisture. Measure and cut the insulation with a utility knife. Glue it in place with construction adhesive.

Garden Bench

Imagine sipping a glass of lemonade and relaxing on this cedar bench some lazy summer afternoon. All it takes is a good day in the shop to make this vision a reality. The bench is designed to be easy to build, so you won't spend hours cutting and sanding elaborate curved profiles. In fact, most of your cutting chores involve making simple crosscuts with a circular saw.

TYPE: Outdoor bench

OVERALL SIZE: 58½L by 33H by 24½D

MATERIAL: Cedar

JOINERY: Butt joints reinforced with glue and screws

CONSTRUCTION DETAILS:
· Project parts are sized to match nominal lumber width and thickness dimensions
· Stainless-steel screws are recommended for assembling the bench in order to avoid black stains around the fastener heads over time

FINISH: Clear wood preservative; could also be left unfinished and allowed to "weather" naturally to a silvery gray color

BUILDING TIME: 6-8 hours

Shopping List

☐ (1) 1 × 6 in. × 8 ft. cedar
☐ (3) 1 × 6 in. × 10 ft. cedar
☐ (5) 2 × 4 in. × 8 ft. cedar
☐ (1) 2 × 6 in. × 8 ft. cedar
☐ #8 stainless-steel deck screws (2-, 2½-, 3-in.)
☐ Finishing materials (optional)

Garden Bench: Step-by-step

BUILD THE BENCH SEAT

❶ Crosscut the seat frame front, back, ends and two stretchers to length, according to the *Cutting List* dimensions on page 146.

❷ Assemble the seat frame front, back and ends. Arrange these parts so the outside faces of the frame ends are flush with the ends of the frame front and back pieces. Clamp up the parts. Drill countersunk pilot holes through the frame front and back pieces into the frame ends, and fasten the parts with 3-in. deck screws.

PHOTO A: Build the bench seat frame by fastening the front, back, ends and two stretchers together with 3-in. countersunk deck screws.

Garden Bench

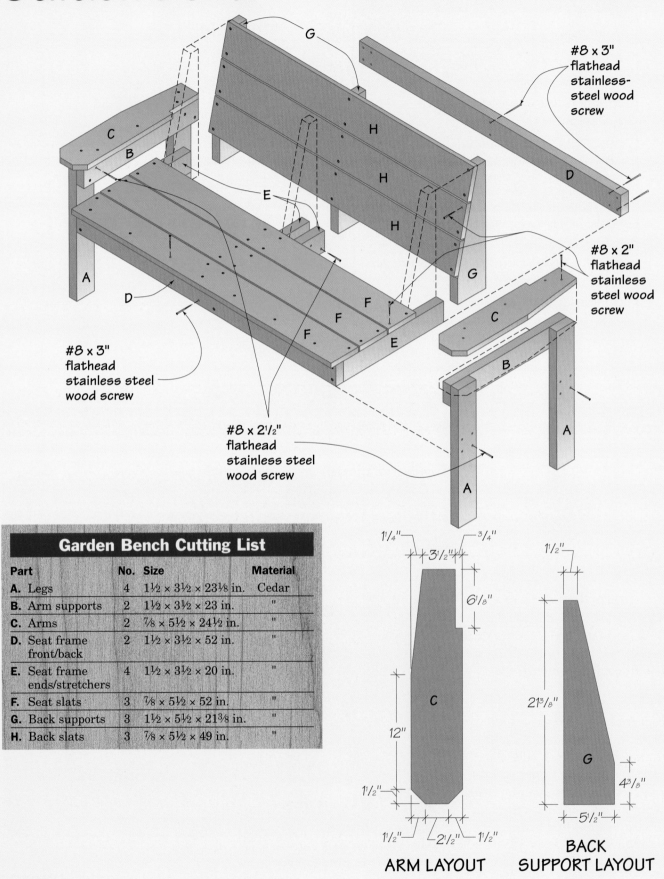

#8 x 3" flathead stainless-steel wood screw

#8 x 2" flathead stainless steel wood screw

#8 x 3" flathead stainless steel wood screw

#8 x 2½" flathead stainless steel wood screw

C

B

A

D

G

H

H

H

E

F

F

F

F

E

G

C

B

A

A

D

Garden Bench Cutting List

Part	No.	Size	Material
A. Legs	4	1½ × 3½ × 23⅛ in.	Cedar
B. Arm supports	2	1½ × 3½ × 23 in.	"
C. Arms	2	⅞ × 5½ × 24½ in.	"
D. Seat frame front/back	2	1½ × 3½ × 52 in.	"
E. Seat frame ends/stretchers	4	1½ × 3½ × 20 in.	"
F. Seat slats	3	⅞ × 5½ × 52 in.	"
G. Back supports	3	1½ × 5½ × 21⅜ in.	"
H. Back slats	3	⅞ × 5½ × 49 in.	"

1¼" 3½" ¾"

6⅛"

C

12"

1½"

1½" 2½" 1½"

ARM LAYOUT

1½"

21³⁄₈"

G

4³⁄₈"

5½"

BACK SUPPORT LAYOUT

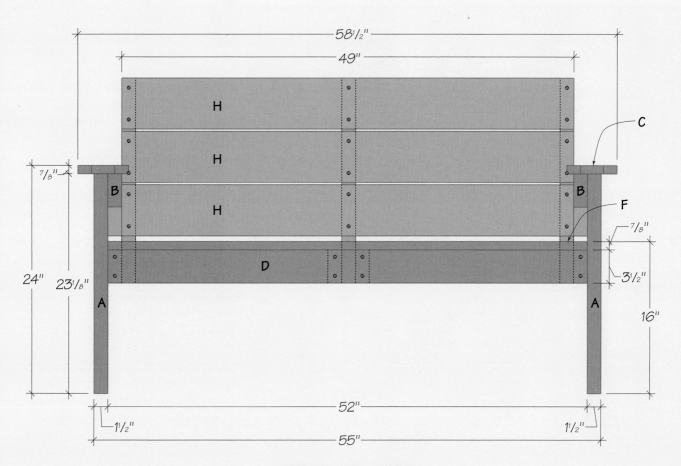

FRONT ELEVATION

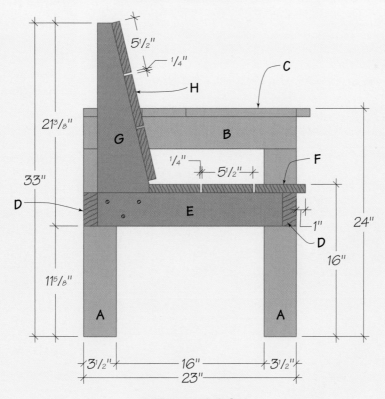

SIDE SECTION

PHOTO B: Install the seat slats on the bench seat frame with screws. Position the back seat slat 7 in. from the back of the seat frame. Insert ¼-in. temporary spacers between the slats before screwing the slats in place.

PHOTO C: Lay out the angled profile on the back support blanks with a straightedge.

PHOTO D: Cut the back supports to shape with your saw guided against a straightedge.

3 Install the two seat frame stretchers: Measure and mark stretcher locations so the stretchers are centered on the width of the frame and spaced 1½ in. apart (this spacing provides clearance for a seat back support later). Drive 3-in. countersunk deck screws through the seat frame front and back to secure the stretchers (**See Photo A**).

4 Crosscut three seat slats to length and fasten them to the seat frame. Arrange the seat slats so the ends are flush with the ends of the seat frame. Space the back slat 7 in. from the back of the frame, and insert ¼-in.-thick scrap spacers between the slats. Once the slats are positioned on the frame, the front slat should overhang the frame by 1 in. Drill countersunk pilot holes through the slats and into the seat frame members, and fasten the slats with 2-in. deck screws (**See Photo B**).

MAKE THE BENCH BACK
5 Lay out the back supports: Crosscut three back support blanks to a length of 21⅜ in. Draw the angled profile on each blank to match the *Back Support Layout* drawing, page 146 (**See Photo C**).

6 Cut the back supports to shape. The easiest way to do this is to clamp each back support to your workbench so the cutting line overhangs the bench. Make the angled rip cuts with your saw guided against a clamped straightedge (**See Photo D**).

7 Crosscut three back slats to length.

8 Assemble the bench back: Arrange the back supports on

your workbench so they rest on their long back edges. Set the back slats in place on the back supports so the top slat on the bench back aligns with the top inside corners of the back supports. Separate the back slats with ¼-in. spacers. The ends of the back slats should be even with the outer back supports. Center the middle back support between the other two supports. Drive pairs of 2-in. deck screws through the slats at each back support location **(See Photo E)**.

ATTACH THE SEAT & BACK

9 Slip the bench back supports inside the bench seat frame, behind the back seat slat and so the center seat stretchers "sandwich" the middle back support. Attach the bench seat and back assemblies by driving pairs of countersunk deck screws through the seat frame back and stretchers and into the back supports **(See Photo F)**.

BUILD THE ARM & LEG ASSEMBLIES

10 Crosscut the four legs and two arm supports to length.

11 Assemble the arm supports and legs: Lay an arm support on each pair of legs with the legs lying flat on the workbench and parallel to each other. Align each arm support so one edge is flush with the ends of the legs. Drive two countersunk screws through the arm supports at each leg to attach the parts and form two leg assemblies **(See Photo G)**.

12 Fasten the leg assemblies to the bench seat: Clamp a leg assembly to each end of the bench seat so the outer edges of the legs are flush with the front and back of the seat. The arm supports

PHOTO E: Attach the back slats along the angled edges of the back supports with screws. Use ¼-in. spacers between the back slats to hold the slats apart.

PHOTO F: Fasten the bench back to the seat by slipping the back supports inside the seat frame and between the stretchers, then screwing through the seat frame back and stretchers into the back supports.

PHOTO G: Make the leg assemblies by fastening each arm support to a pair of legs. Drive pairs of 2½-in. countersunk deck screws through the arm supports and into each leg.

PHOTO H: Position and clamp the leg assemblies to the ends of the bench seat and attach the parts with screws. The arm supports should face inward.

should face inward. Adjust the parts so the seat slats are 16 in. up from the leg bottoms. Fasten the legs to the bench seat with four 2½-in. deck screws at each leg (See Photo H).

MAKE & ATTACH THE ARMS

⑬ Crosscut two 24½-in. boards for the arms. Refer to the *Arm Layout* drawing, page 146, to draw the arm shapes on the blanks (See Photo I).

⑭ Clamp each arm workpiece to your worksurface, and cut out the arm shapes with a jig saw (See Photo J).

⑮ Position the arms on the arm supports so the back ends of the arms are flush with the back edges of the back legs. The long notch on each arm should wrap around the back supports, and the inside edge of the arms should overhang the arm supports by ¾ in. Attach the arms to the leg assemblies with 2-in. countersunk deck screws (See Photo K).

FINISHING TOUCHES

⑯ Sand all of the bench surfaces and ease the corners and edges with 100-grit sandpaper, especially the seat and back slats as well as the arms (See Photo L).

⑰ Brush on several coats of clear wood preservative, if you wish.

PHOTO I: Lay out the arm shapes on a pair of 1 × 6 cedar boards.

PHOTO J: Cut out the arms with a jig saw, with the workpieces clamped to your workbench.

PHOTO K: Position the arms on the leg assemblies and fasten them to the arm supports and the legs with screws.

PHOTO L: Sand the bench smooth, especially the seat and back slats as well as the arms. Cedar dust can be a respiratory irritant, so wear a dust mask when sanding.

Two-step Stool

Those top-shelf items will always be within easy reach if you keep this step stool near the kitchen or pantry. The steps are made with pre-milled oak stair treads, so they're strong as well as attractive, and the 17 × 18-in. stool base will keep you surefooted even with both feet on the top step.

Vital statistics

TYPE: Two-step stool

OVERALL SIZE: 18L by 15H by 17D

MATERIAL: Birch plywood, oak stair tread

JOINERY: Butt joints reinforced with glue and screws

CONSTRUCTION DETAILS:
- Sides joined to stretchers with screws to strengthen the stool and to keep it from racking
- Handle cutout in top step made by drilling out the ends of the cutout with a spade bit, then removing the waste between the holes with a jig saw
- Sides are made of plywood to eliminate the need for gluing up solid-wood panels

FINISH: Primer and paint; varnish

BUILDING TIME: 3-4 hours

Shopping List

- ☐ (1) ¾ in. × 2 × 4 ft. birch plywood
- ☐ (1) 1 × 12 × 36 in. bullnosed oak stair tread
- ☐ #8 × 2-in. flathead wood screws
- ☐ 2-in. finish nails
- ☐ Wood glue
- ☐ Finishing materials

Two-step Stool: Step-by-step

MAKE THE STRETCHERS

❶ Lay out and cut the back stretchers: Rip two 2-in.-wide, 2-ft.-long strips from the plywood sheet. Make these rip cuts with your saw guided against a straightedge. Then crosscut the strips into 15-in.-long stretchers.

❷ Lay out and cut the front stretchers: The stretcher beneath the front edge of each step receives a decorative angled cutout along the bottom edge. Since these stretchers are only 2 in. wide, it wouldn't be safe or easy to make the angled cutouts after ripping

PHOTO A: Gang-cut the stool sides to shape, following the cutting lines you drew on the top workpiece. Use a stiff, fine-toothed blade in the jig saw to produce accurate, smooth cuts. Guide the saw against a clamped straightedge for best results.

Two-step Stool

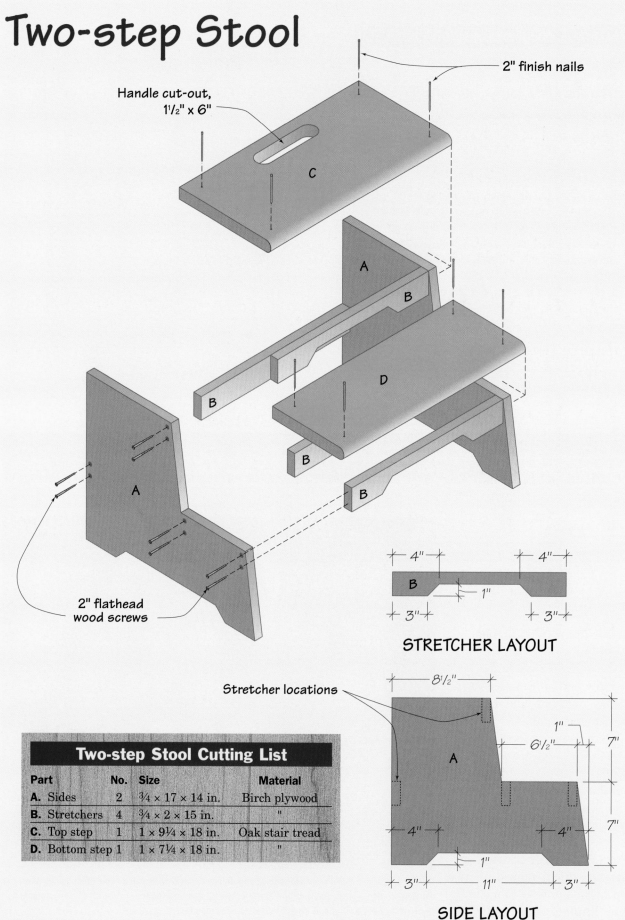

Handle cut-out,
1½" x 6"

2" finish nails

C

A

B

B

A

D

B

B

B

2" flathead
wood screws

4"   4"

B

1"

3"   3"

STRETCHER LAYOUT

Stretcher locations

8½"

1"

6½"   7"

A

4"   4"

1"   7"

3"   11"   3"

SIDE LAYOUT

Two-step Stool Cutting List

Part	No.	Size	Material
A. Sides	2	¾ × 17 × 14 in.	Birch plywood
B. Stretchers	4	¾ × 2 × 15 in.	"
C. Top step	1	1 × 9¼ × 18 in.	Oak stair tread
D. Bottom step	1	1 × 7¼ × 18 in.	"

and crosscutting the stretchers to size. Instead, make the two stretchers one at a time, laying out and cutting the angled profile into the large sheet of plywood first, then cutting the stretcher free. For each stretcher, draw the angled cutout along the end of the plywood sheet, using the *Stretcher Layout* drawing, page 154, as a guide. Cut out the profile with a jig saw. Then measure and mark the length and width of the stretcher around the cutout, and rip and crosscut the stretcher to size.

MAKE THE SIDES

❸ Rip and crosscut two plywood pieces for the stool sides.

❹ Draw the sides: Since the proportions of both side panels match, you can draw the shape of a side onto one board, stack the boards on top of one another and cut them both to size at one time. Use the *Side Layout* drawing, page 154, as a guide for laying out the profile.

❺ Cut out the sides. Clamp the plywood together so the leg shapes are in the same arrangement. Cut both sides to shape with a jig saw **(See Photo A).**

ASSEMBLE THE SIDES & STRETCHERS

❻ Mark the positions of the stretchers on the side panels: The top edge of the back stretcher is 7 in. up from the bottom of each side. The stretchers with profiles should align with the top front edges of the steps. The remaining stretcher supports the back edge of the bottom step.

❼ Fasten the sides and stretchers together: Spread glue on the ends of the stretchers and within the stretcher locations on the sides.

PHOTO B: Glue and clamp the stretchers in place between the stool sides. Fasten the parts with countersunk flathead wood screws.

PHOTO C: Conceal the screwheads and any voids in the plywood with wood putty, spreading the putty with a putty knife. Once the putty dries, sand away the excess.

PHOTO D: Measure, mark and rip-cut both oak steps to width. Be sure to clamp the workpieces securely to your worksurface when making the cuts.

PHOTO E: Remove the waste within the handle cutout area on the top step. We drilled out the rounded ends of the cutout first with a 1½-in.-dia. spade bit, then cut away the rest of the waste with a jig saw.

Clamp the stretchers in place between the sides. Drill pairs of countersunk pilot holes through the sides and into the stretchers, then drive 2-in. flathead wood screws to secure the parts **(See Photo B).**

FINISH THE STOOL BASE

8 Fill the holes left by the screw-heads with wood putty **(See Photo C).** Fill any voids in the edges of the plywood parts with putty as well.

9 Sand the exposed surfaces of the stool base with 150-grit sandpaper to smooth the puttied areas and ease the edges.

10 Prime and paint the stool base, but leave the top edges of the sides and stretchers bare for glue in areas that will be covered by the oak stair treads.

MAKE THE STAIR TREADS

11 Cut the 36-in. length of oak stair tread in half to make the 18-in.-long stool steps.

12 Rip-cut the top and bottom steps to width: Mark the top step to a width of 9¼ in. and the bottom step to 7¼ in. Lay out these cuts so you'll trim off the edge opposite the bullnosed (rounded-over) edge. Clamp each step to your worksurface, and guide the saw against a straightedge when ripping the steps to width **(See Photo D).**

13 Lay out and cut the handle cutout in the top step: The handle cutout is 6 in. long and 1½ in. wide, with rounded ends. Position the cutout so it is centered on the length of the top step and inset 1 in. from the back edge. There are several ways to remove the waste from the cutout: You could drill a small pilot hole within the waste area for starting the saw blade, and cut away all of the waste with a jig saw. However, the tight end radii would be difficult to cut without needing plenty of sanding afterward. A better option is to drill out the curved ends of the cutout with a 1½-in. spade bit, then remove the remaining waste with a jig saw **(See Photo E).** The second method ensures that the rounded ends of the cutout will be uniform and smooth. Once you've removed the waste, file and sand the edges of the cutout smooth.

INSTALL THE STEPS

⑭ Position the oak steps on the stool base and mark the overhang on the ends. The back edge of the top step should align with the back edge of the stool. The bottom step should seat fully on the lower flat surface on the stool sides. Both steps overhang the stool base by ¾ in. on each side. Clamp the steps in place on the stool base.

⑮ Fasten the steps to the stool base. Drill pilot holes for 2-in. finish nails, positioning the nails so the steps will attach to both the stool sides and stretchers **(See Photo F).** Remove the clamps and spread glue on the mating surfaces of the parts. Re-clamp the steps on the stool base and nail the steps in place. Recess the nailheads **(See Photo G).**

FINISH THE STEPS

⑯ Fill holes left by the nailheads in the steps with tinted wood putty. Sand the putty and the steps smooth and ease any other sharp edges.

⑰ Apply several coats of a clear finish, like polyurethane, to all exposed surfaces of the steps.

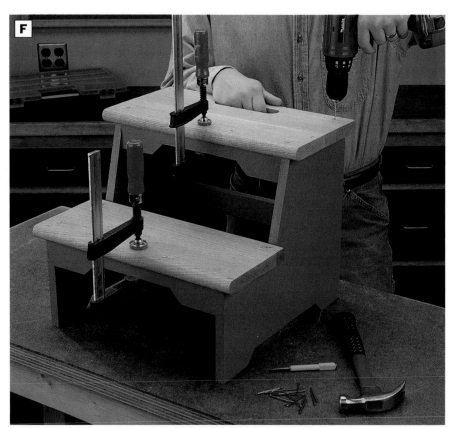

PHOTO F: Clamp the steps in place on the stool base. Drill pilot holes through the steps and into the stretchers and sides for attaching the parts with 2-in. finish nails.

PHOTO G: Recess the nailheads with a nailset. Conceal the holes with wood putty tinted to match the oak steps.

Index

Index of Projects